The Story of Commodore John Barry

Martin I. J. Griffin

ESPRIOS.COM
ESPRIOS DIGITAL PUBLISHING

COMMODORE BARRY
(After Chappelle)

"I serve the country for nothing" —BARRY

"May a suitable recompense always attend your bravery" —WASHINGTON

THE STORY

OF

COMMODORE JOHN BARRY

"Father of the American Navy"

BY

MARTIN I.J. GRIFFIN

Historian of the Society of the Friendly Sons of St. Patrick
of Philadelphia

PHILADELPHIA

1908

Dedicated

TO

The Society of the Friendly Sons of St. Patrick
for the Relief of Emigrants from Ireland

The Story of Commodore John Barry

CHAPTER I.

His Naval Renown—His Career in the Colonial Mercantile Marine Service—Appointed to the "Lexington" by the Continental Marine Committee—His First Cruise.

The American Navy by its achievements has won enduring fame and imperishable honor. The careers of many of its heroes have been narrated fully, and oft in fulsome terms. All Americans unite in these tributes of praise where justly due.

JOHN BARRY has, aptly and justly, been called "THE FATHER OF THE AMERICAN NAVY." His early, constant and worthy services in defence of our country; his training many of those who became the foremost and most distinguished sons of the sea in our early naval annals makes the title one fitly bestowed.

The Congress of his country having directed the erection in the Capital City of the Nation of a monument commemorative of the man and his deeds, this is a fitting time to present a brief record of his career and of his deeds during the Revolutionary War, which won the Independence of our Country, and also in the War with France, which maintained the integrity of the new Nation and the protection of its commerce. In both wars he bore a heroic part. At all times his services were useful and brilliant.

"Captain John Barry may justly be considered the Father of our Navy," wrote Mr. Dennie in *The Portfolio*, July 1813, in giving the first biographical sketch of this distinguished naval officer. "The utility of whose services and the splendor of whose exploits entitle him to the foremost rank among our naval heroes."

Allen's *Biographical Dictionary*, published in 1809, declared he "was a patriot of integrity and unquestioned bravery."

Frost's *Naval Biography* states: "Few commanders were employed in a greater variety of services or met the enemy under greater disadvantages," and yet he did not fail to acquit himself of his duty in a manner becoming a skillful seaman and a brave warrior.

THE BARONY OF FORTH

"His public services were not limited to any customary rule of professional duty, but without regard to labor, danger or excuses, his devotion to his Country kept him constantly engaged in acts of public utility. The regard and admiration of General Washington, which he possessed in an eminent degree, were among the most eminent fruits of his patriotic career."

The Story of Commodore John Barry

Judson's *Sages and Heroes of the Revolution* says: "Barry was noble in spirit, humane in discipline, discreet and fearless in battle, urbane in his manners, a splendid officer, a good citizen, a devoted Christian and a true Patriot."

Many other quotations might be cited to show the high esteem in which Commodore John Barry was held as well also the importance of his services to our Country.

A brief narration of his career will set forth the character and worth of these services as well as afford proof of the valor and fidelity of this most successful naval officer.

BALLYSAMPSON

John Barry was born in 1745 in the townland of Ballysampson. He lived his boyhood in the townland of Roostoonstown, both in the parish of Tacumshin, Barony of Forth, Province of Leinster in Ireland. The parish covers three thousand acres. It is situated between two townland-locked gulfs with very narrow openings— Lake Tacumshin and Lady's Island Lake. Possibly these lakes gave young Barry the inspiration for the sea, and upon both he in youth, we may be sure, oft pulled the oar.

The Story of Commodore John Barry

When and under what circumstances young Barry left his birthplace and departed from Ireland are not known. The best traditionary evidence justifies us in believing that leaving Ireland, while yet young, he went to Spanishtown in the Island of Jamaica and from there, when about fifteen years of age, came to Philadelphia, where he found employment in the commercial fleets of Samuel Meredith and of Willing & Morris, leaders in the mercantile life of the city.

TACUMSHIN LOUGH

LADY'S ISLAND LOUGH

The Story of Commodore John Barry

Being but a boy, records do not attest his presence or position. But however lowly, we are sure that merit hovered over every action and proved the worth of the young navigator of the seas so fully that on attaining his twenty-first year he was at once entrusted with the sole command of a vessel—the schooner "Barbadoes," sixty tons, which cleared from Philadelphia on October 2, 1766.

The schooner he commanded was registered at the Custom House on September 29, 1766. It was built at Liverpool, in the Province of Nova Scotia and was owned by Edward Denny, of Philadelphia. John Barry was registered as its Captain.

In this schooner, small in measurement and in tonnage by the standard of our times and yet not surpassed in either by many vessels in the colonial marine trade, John Barry, now a man in years and capabilities, continued until early in 1771 to make voyages to and from Bridgetown, the principal port of Barbadoes.

BRIDGETOWN

In May, 1771, he became Captain of the brig "Patty and Polly," sailing from St. Croix to Philadelphia. In August of that year we find him Captain of the schooner "Industry," of forty-five tons, plying to and from Virginia, making trips to New York, voyages to Nevis and to and from Halifax, Nova Scotia until, on October 9, 1772, he became Commander of the "Peggy" sailing to and from St. Eustatia and Montserrat until, on December 19, 1774, a register for the ship the "Black Prince" was issued to John Barry as Master. It was owned

The Story of Commodore John Barry

by John Nixon, whose grandfather, Richard, a Catholic, of Barry's own county, Wexford, arrived in Philadelphia in 1686. John Nixon read the Declaration of Independence on July 8, 1776. On December 21st Barry sailed to Bristol, where he arrived at the end of January, 1775. Later he proceeded to London, where he arrived June 7th, from whence he returned to Philadelphia, where he arrived October 13th, the very day Congress had resolved to fit out two armed cruisers, one of fourteen guns and one of ten guns, the first act founding a Continental naval force for the United Colonies.

The Marine Committee, under the authority of this Resolve of the Continental Congress, purchased two vessels and named one the "Lexington," the other the "Reprisal."

To the "Lexington" John Barry was commissioned Captain on December 7, 1775. Captain Wickes was the same day named Commander of the "Reprisal."

Barry's vessel the "Black Prince," the finest vessel engaged in the Colonial commerce, was purchased by the Marine Committee, renamed the "Alfred," after Alfred the Great, the founder of the English Navy. To the "Alfred" John Paul Jones was appointed Lieutenant under Captain Salstonstall, on the same day Barry and Wickes were appointed Captains.

The "Lexington" and the "Reprisal" were separate and independent commands under direct orders of the Marine Committee and not subject to, nor were they part of, the fleet under Commodore Hopkins. Captain John Barry was thus the first Commander appointed under the direct authority of the Continental Congress. He was appointed to the first Continental armed cruiser—the "Lexington"—named after the first battle place of the Revolution. It was the first vessel fitted out under Continental authority by the Marine Committee and "in the nature of things was more readily equipped" than the "Alfred," says Cooper's *History of the Navy*. This was especially so as Willing & Morris, Captain Barry's late employers, alone had a stock of "round shot for four pounders,

The Story of Commodore John Barry

under their store in Penn Street and in their yard." These were readily available to Captain Barry of the "Lexington."

When Barry's cruiser was ready for sea the severity of the weather in blocking the Delaware with ice debarred its passage to the Bay and out into the Ocean. In the meanwhile Barry was busily employed on shore duty and in assisting in preparing the fleet of Commodore Hopkins for its departure on February 17, 1776, on its expedition to the Southward. This fleet was intended for the protection of American vessels off the coast of Virginia, but it proceeded to the Bahama Islands. On St. Patrick's Day, 1776, Hopkins sailed from New Providence bringing the Governor and others as hostages as well as securing military stores and ammunition. Washington on the same day was entering the City of Boston on its forced evacuation by the British.

Meanwhile Captain John Barry was busy in constant service on the Delaware River and on shore, promoting the progress of naval affairs conducive to the formation of a navy.

It was not, however, until March 23d that Congress ordered Letters of Marque to be issued and authorized public and private cruisers to capture British vessels or to seize or destroy supplies for the British naval forces.

Captain Barry, in the "Lexington," at once proceeded down the Delaware. On March 29, 1776, was off Cape May, New Jersey. On Sunday, the 31st, the "Lexington" went out to sea—his first entry upon the watery domain bearing the flag of defiance—the Union or Continental flag hoisted at Cambridge on January 1, 1776, by General Washington, which he had adopted so that "our vessels may know one another," and so "distinguish our friends from our foes," as he had written Captain Barry's friend and fellow-Catholic of Philadelphia, Colonel Stephen Moylan, the Muster Master General of his army.

When Captain Barry proceeded to sea, the "Roebuck," British man-of-war, "one of His Majesty's pirates" and her tender, the "Edward," "put to sea" also after the "Lexington," but Barry was too swift and got so far away that the "Roebuck" returned the same evening to the Bay.

Barry's historical and patriotic career had begun.

ADMIRALTY SEAL AND SIGNATURE OF THE SECRETARY OF THE BOARD

CHAPTER II.

CAPTURES THE "EDWARD"—HIS PRISONER RICHARD DALE—IMPORTANCE OF THE PRIZE—BARRY UNKNOWN TO OR IGNORED BY CAPTAIN HOBSON.

The "Lexington" cruised off the coast of Virginia a week without meeting with the enemy. Barry had gone to sea on Sunday. The Sunday following, April 7, 1776, while off the "Capes of Virginia" he "fell in with the sloop 'Edward' belonging to the 'Liverpool' frigate" and "shattered her in a terrible manner," as he reported to the Marine Committee, after an engagement of "near two glasses." The "Lexington" lost two men killed and two wounded. The "Edward" had "several of her crew killed and wounded." She carried "eight guns and a number of swivels" and was commanded by Lieutenant Richard Boger of the "Liverpool." Barry brought the "shattered" captive to Philadelphia with the crew of twenty-five prisoners taken.

Among the number was Richard Dale, of Virginia, who had been Lieutenant of a light cruiser in the service of Virginia, which had been captured by the "Edward." Dale was "induced to adopt the Royal cause" and so took service on the "Edward" and so was taken prisoner.

Captain Barry induced young Dale to return to American allegiance and accept service under him on the "Lexington" as Midshipman. Dale in October, when the "Lexington" was assigned to Captain Johnston, became Master's Mate. He continued in the service of the United Colonies and rose to be a Commodore in the Navy under the present Constitution. He ever retained the friendship of Captain Barry, who, by his will, bequeathed to his "good friend, Captain Richard Dale, his gold-hilted sword as a token of his esteem."

This sword had been presented to John Paul Jones by King Louis XVI after the memorable battle between the "Bonne Homme Richard" commanded by Jones and the "Serapis," as the expedition commanded by Jones was under French auspices and direction. The sword "was sent by Jones' heirs to Robert Morris," the financier of the Revolution, "who presented it to Commodore John Barry, the senior officer of the present American Navy, who will never disgrace it," Morris wrote, March 18, 1795, to Thomas Pinckney, the American Minister to Great Britain. Barry by his will bequeathed it to "my good friend Captain Richard Dale," with whose descendants it yet remains. It is claimed by the Morris family that the gift to Barry was "in trust to descend to the senior officer of the Navy." There is no proof of the trust nor is there any that Jones' heirs gave the sword of great money value to Morris. Morris had it. He gave it to Barry who bequeathed it to Dale who, two months before Barry made his will, had resigned from the Navy. There could have been no "trust" for Barry to "disregard." But it is singular that it is now possessed by those whose ancestor had, by Barry, been induced to return to American allegiance after having entered the service of the enemy.

The "Edward," taken by Barry, was the first armed vessel taken under the authority of the Continental Marine Committee and brought to Philadelphia, the seat of Congress, and delivered to its Marine Committee. Previous captures off the New England coast by Manly and others, had been those of unarmed supply vessels to Quebec or Boston under authority of General Washington. The capture was most important. When the project had, in August, 1775, been presented to Congress by the delegates from Rhode Island, by direction of its Assembly, to fit out armed cruisers, many of the patriots thought it of doubtful wisdom to do so against the powerful British Navy. Samuel Chase, of Maryland, declared "it is the maddest idea in the world."

So Barry's capture was a demonstration of the ability of the Colonies to contest the sea with Great Britain and to do it so effectively that "we captured from the British over eight hundred vessels and more than twelve thousand seamen, and of these more than one hundred were war vessels of the Royal Navy, carrying more than two thousand, five hundred guns, while the American losses were scarcely more than one-sixth those of the British," as Captain Richmond Pearson Hobson declared in an address on the Navy on Flag Day, 1901, at the Buffalo Pan-American Exposition. Yet he, in looking "over the range of our Naval history, saw a long line of majestic figures whose very names are an inspiration," did not, in giving the names of twenty-one of these "majestic figures," name Captain John Barry, the very "Father of the Navy." He was not mentioned as among those which "History with her bright and luminous pencil inscribed upon the glorious scroll." Captain Hobson, the heroic, is now a member of Congress from Alabama and ought to make reparation for his ignorance or conscious ignoring of the foremost naval commander of the very Navy he proved himself to be a worthy representative of. He may become unknown or be ignored if known.

Captain Barry had command of the first Continental cruiser, the "Lexington," and the last frigate, the "Alliance"—the largest and finest vessel in the Revolutionary Navy—had made the first capture under Continental authority and fought the last battle of the Revolution, and commanded the whole of the Navy at the close of the war—had been the earliest, the constant and the latest fighter and the first Captain and ranking officer of the present Navy on its establishment in 1794. Yet he was entirely unknown to Captain Hobson. Or was he purposely ignored?

The capture of the "Edward" was considered of considerable import in patriot circles: "We begin to make some little figure here in the navy way," wrote John Adams, the day after the arrival of Barry and his prize. The Marine Committee also wrote to Commodore Hopkins, who had arrived at New London, Connecticut, the same day Barry had arrived at Philadelphia with his prize, informing him of the capture and saying the loss to the British of the twenty-five men was one "they cannot easily provide against—the want of men."

The demonstration of satisfaction at Philadelphia because of Barry's success gave heart to the patriots in an endeavor to have an increase in the naval force. By the alertness of armed cruisers, protection would be given to the supplies coming to the Americans and at the same time captures could be made of supplies going to the British.

The Story of Commodore John Barry

On May 1, 1776, the "Edward," condemned by the Court of Admiralty as a prize to the "Lexington'" was, with all her ammunition, furniture, tackle and apparel, sold at public auction and the proceeds divided between the Government and Captain Barry and his crew.

CHAPTER III.

BARRY APPOINTED TO COMMAND DEFENSIVE OPERATIONS IN DELAWARE BAY AND RIVER—CAPTURES BRITISH SUPPLIES AND PROTECTS AMERICAN—SAVES THE CARGO OF THE "NANCY" AND EXPLODES HER WHEN THE BRITISH BOARD HER—CAPTURES THE "LADY SUSAN" AND THE "BETSY"—APPOINTED TO THE "EFFINGHAM."

The "Lexington" was not in a condition to then proceed on another expedition, as she needed fitting up. Yet Captain Barry was not permitted to be idle. On May 8th, Robert Morris, for the Marine Committee of Congress, directed him to go down the Delaware River in the sloop "Hornet," commanded by Captain Hallock, and to take the officers and men of the "Lexington" to supply the Provincial armed ship, commanded by Captain Read, the Floating Battery and the "Reprisal," under Captain Wickes, with men sufficient to have these vessels "fit for immediate action," and to give the "utmost exertions" of himself, officers and men in defending the pass at Fort Island so as to prevent the British coming to Philadelphia; and also to take, sink or destroy such as attempted to do so as well as pursue those he thought it advisable to follow. This made Captain Barry the Commodore or ranking officer in the naval operations in Delaware Bay. The next day Captain Barry reported to Mr. Morris, urging the fitting out of the "Lexington" so "she might be of service. The more there is the better," said the Captain, though adding, "We shall keep them in play."

So the "Lexington" was fitted out and sent down the Bay to Barry where the "Roebuck" and "Liverpool," British frigates, were "in and about." Barry joined the rest of the fleet at Cape May. The "Liverpool" "was scared away" when the Americans went "in quest of the pirates."

At this time the thirteen vessels ordered in December to be built for the Marine Committee were being completed at Philadelphia, Boston and Baltimore. Captain Barry was appointed to the command of one being built at Philadelphia—the "Effingham" being assigned him in October.

All the while, however, Barry was in command of the "Lexington" in the Delaware Bay and off the Capes, giving protection to the Continental supply vessels coming to Philadelphia, which had been sent out for necessaries. One arrived at Philadelphia with 7,400 pounds of powder as well as a number of firearms. Barry also sent up to Philadelphia the war stores he captured. On June 12, 1776, the Secret Committee of Congress directed that Colonel Megraw's Battalion be given the 191 firearms "sent up by Captain Barry." She narrowly escaped capture by the "Liverpool," but two of the Continental vessels protected her and a French schooner. Other French vessels from the West Indies, bringing molasses, coffee, linen and other supplies were also saved from capture by Captain Barry and the other Continental and Provincial commanders under his authority. On June 10th the "Kingfisher," British man-of-war, captured a brigantine from Wilmington, but "before the pirate boarded her our brave Captain Barry had been on board of her and taken out some powder and arms," was the report Henry Fisher, of Lewistown, sent the Committee of Safety by whale-boat to New Castle and thence by land because the Tories of the County had cut off all horse express communication.

The tenders of the "Roebuck," the "Liverpool" and the "Kingfisher" attempted to seize the cattle and stock which the Tories had stored for the British at Indian River, "but were prevented by Barry's brig," as they called her, thus indicating that the alertness and success of the "brave Captain Barry" had become conspicuously known to the Tories of lower Delaware, a nest of Loyalists.

The brig "Nancy" bringing supplies from St. Croix and St. Thomas for Congress account and having 386 barrels of gunpowder, 50 firelocks, 101 hogsheads of rum, 62 of sugar and bales of dry goods, on June 29, 1776, while making for Cape May, was pursued by six British men-of-war but, getting assistance from Captain Barry's "Lexington," she was run ashore and 268 barrels of the powder and most of the other stores saved. Powder was, by Barry's order, placed in the cabin and in the mainsail, in the folds of which fire was put. The British boarded the brig. An explosion soon took place and "blew the pirates into the air." It "was supposed forty or fifty were destroyed by the explosion."

On July 2, 1776, the day the Resolution declared the Colonies free and independent, John Hancock, President of the Congress so declaring, notified Captain Barry that as "the frigate you are to command is not yet launched, her guns and anchors not yet ready," it was but "a piece of justice due to your merit to allow you to make a cruise in the 'Lexington' for one or two months, in hopes that fortune may favor your industry and reward it with some good prizes." On this cruise Barry met that "fortune" which his industry merited. He captured several prizes of which record have been discovered.

SIGNATURES TO BARRY'S ORDERS

On August 2d the "Lady Susan," "an armed vessel, was taken by Captain Barry at sea," reported Cæsar Rodney to his brother at Dover the next day. This was "a privateer of eight four-pound carriage guns commanded by another of those famous Goodriches of Virginia." She was loaded with naval stores from Bermuda. After an "obstinate engagement" of an hour and a half "she struck." Nearly all of her crew of twenty-five after their capture took service under Barry.

The "Betsy," a sloop of fifty tons, commanded by Samuel Kerr, was also at this time captured by the "Lexington" under Barry. Both prizes were condemned to Captain Barry on September 26th by the Court of Admiralty, but an appeal in the case of the "Betsy" was taken to Congress.

The newly built "Effingham" being ready, Captain Barry surrendered, on October 18, 1776, the "Lexington" to Captain Henry Johnston and took command of the "Effingham," named in honor of Lord Effingham, who had resigned his commission in the British Army rather than take arms against the Colonies, because of his "strict adherence to those principles of the Revolution of 1688," which he declared the Colonies were contending for and for so doing the merchants of Dublin, on July 17, 1775, approved of his conduct in "honestly and spiritedly resigning," and for his "noble efforts in support of American Liberty."

CHAPTER IV.

BARRY APPOINTED TO THE "EFFINGHAM"—THE QUESTION OF RANK—BARRY ENGAGES IN THE TRENTON CAMPAIGN—AN AIDE TO WASHINGTON AND TO CADWALLADER—COMMANDER OF THE PORT OF PHILADELPHIA—STRIKE OF THE NAVY LIEUTENANTS—OPERATIONS OF BARRY ON THE DELAWARE.

A reorganization of the Navy of the United Colonies took place on October 10, 1776, when assignments were made of the several armed vessels then belonging to the "United States," as that was the title Congress had, on September 9th, ordered to be used in all public documents. The order in which these assignments were made was generally regarded as fixing the rank of each Captain. So it occasioned agitation and discussion. It was not, however, officially stated that such was the case. Later it was declared not to be so by Committee of Congress.

Captain John Barry was assigned to No. 7 on the list. Those preceding him were: (1) James Nicholson, to the "Virginia," 28 guns; (2) John Manly, to the "Hancock," 32 guns; (3) Hector McNeil, to the "Boston," 24 guns; (4) Dudley Salstonstall, to the "Trumbull," 28 guns; (5) Nicholas Biddle, to the "Randolph," 32 guns; (6) Thomas Thompson, to the "Raleigh," 32 guns; (7) John Barry, to the "Effingham," 28 guns. John Paul Jones was given No. 18. The Marine Committee in making up the list could hardly, in view of the number of guns of the several vessels and the selection of Captains who had not as yet served in the Navy, have intended the position assigned as fixing the official rank of the several officers. James Nicholson, the first named and to a 28-gun ship, had not heretofore been noted for any special services justifying his appointment as the ranking officer of the Navy, though giving him a vessel inferior in armament to others lower in position. Captain John Manly, No. 2, was "uneasy and threatened to resign." He had in New England waters done early and good services. Captain Thompson's friends declared he ought to have been placed higher. Yet Manly and Thompson were given 32-gun ships, while Captain Nicholson, No. 1, was given a 28 and Captain Barry, No. 7, was also given a 28. Captain John Paul Jones, No. 18, ever contested the assignment to that position, declaring that "rank opens the door to glory." As late as 1781 he made contest before Committee of Congress. It reported that though there was, "on October 10, 1776, an arrangement of Captains, the Committee cannot fully ascertain the rule by which that arrangement was made, as the relative rank was not conformable to the times of appointment or dates of commission and seems repugnant to a resolution of December 22, 1775."

Captain Barry appears not to have made any objection to his position on the list. He was ready and eager for service and, seemingly, not concerned as to rank or position. He had been given a vessel equal to Captain Nicholson, No. 1. Those to whom stronger armament had been given had not been early or foremost in service or activity. Some of them did not, later, justify any outranking, if that were the case. Captain Barry was early in the struggle, foremost during its continuance and latest in service.

Jones declared that some gentlemen in the first days of the Navy did not join the Navy as "they did not choose to be hanged, as the hazard was very great." But Captain John Barry did not hesitate. He came quickly from London to engage in the conflict, and from the very first day of his return to America was active in service and on duty. Still rank was not necessary to "open the door to glory," for No. 7 became the chief officer of the Navy and No. 18 achieved imperishable fame and popular renown. The pay of the Captains was sixty dollars a month. The uniform was: Blue cloth with red lapels, slash cuff, stand-up collar, flat yellow buttons, blue breeches, red waistcoat with yellow lace.

Interested in the Navy, Captain Barry was also concerned in affairs on land. So when on November 25, 1776, a meeting was held at the Indian Queen Hotel, Philadelphia, to consider accusations against those "suspected as Tories and unfriendly to the cause of America," Captain Barry was there. We may be sure he was earnest and active in any measures to restrict the operations of those inimicable to Liberty or engaged in efforts detrimental to the Patriots' endeavors.

Captain Barry, on November 30, 1776, united with Captains Biddle, Read, Alexander and John Nicholson in a memorial to Congress. It was referred to the Marine Committee, who were directed to pursue such measures as they might think proper. What the memorial related to has not been discovered after long continued endeavor to ascertain. It is not among the papers of the Continental Congress nor

The Story of Commodore John Barry

mentioned in the records of the Marine Committee, which have been preserved at the Library of Congress.

At this time affairs were serious with General Washington. The battle of Long Island, in August, had been disastrous. Forts Lee and Washington, the bulwarks of the Hudson, had been lost and the sad and gloomy, but marvelously strategic, retreat across New Jersey was being conducted by Washington, pursued by Lord Cornwallis.

Washington "was at the end of the tether." "In ten days this army will have ceased to exist," was his almost despairing cry to Congress, calling for aid to strengthen his disappearing and dispirited army. Yet on the upper Delaware, amid all the encircling gloom, God's precious Providence and love was at no time during the Revolution more strikingly manifested. All seemed lost this bleak December, 1776. The hour of defeat, dismay and destruction seemed about to strike. The timid, the faint-hearted, the treacherous were fast accepting British allegiance. Even heretofore stalwart hearts wavered in the cause of Liberty. The newly proclaimed Independence of hot July, the threat and defiance of the Colonies to England's tyranny, was now in the chill December, like the earth, about to be sheathed in the coldness of death.

The alarm came to Philadelphia. Shops were shut, schools closed and the inhabitants engaged solely in providing for the defense of the City, now the aim of the enemy. But out of all this gloom and alarm came the victory at Trenton.

Captain John Barry organized a company of volunteers and went to Washington's assistance. In cooperation with the marines under Captain William Brown, he lent efficient service in transporting Washington's army across the Delaware prior to the Battle of Trenton. Captain Barry acted as an aide to General Cadwallader, and on one occasion, of which there is record, as an aide to Washington in the safe conduct to Philadelphia of the baggage of the captured Hessians and also of the surgeons and physicians to Princeton.

After the Trenton campaign and its consequent successful results, Captain Barry returned to Philadelphia and engaged in naval preparations for the defense of the city. He was the Senior Commander of the Navy in the Port of Philadelphia.

MISS ELIZABETH ADAMS BARNES
Great-Great-Grandniece of Commodore Barry; who christened "The Barry" Boat March 22, 1902

In July, 1777, twelve of the lieutenants of the fleet under Barry struck for an increase of pay and allowances. They notified Captain Barry they would not act on board any vessel until their grievances were redressed. Barry informed the Marine Committee. It reported the affair to Congress, saying that such a combination of officers was of the "most dangerous tendency." Whereupon the Congress dismissed all of the lieutenants and declared their commissions "void and of no effect." The offenders were declared incapable of holding any commission under the United States and recommending the several States not to employ any in offices civil or military. This brought the lieutenants to "acknowledge in the most explicit manner that the offense for which they were dismissed is highly reprehensible and could not be justified under any circumstances or any pretence whatever, and that they were exceedingly sorry for the rashness which betrayed them into such behavior." Then the strikers were "restored to former rank and command."

CHAPTER V.

THE BRITISH CAPTURE PHILADELPHIA—ACTIVITY OF BARRY—COMMANDER OF NAVY AT PORT OF PHILADELPHIA—BATTLE AT RED BANK—ORDERED BY WASHINGTON AND NAVY BOARD TO SINK THE VESSELS ON THE UPPER DELAWARE—PROTESTS—DECLARED HE KNEW MORE ABOUT A SHIP THAN WASHINGTON AND THE BOARD—CHARGED WITH DISRESPECT—HIS DEFENSE TO CONGRESS—HIS BRILLIANT OPERATIONS ON THE DELAWARE.

The British, in 1776 having failed to reach Philadelphia by the northward way through New Jersey, planned the 1777 campaigns to end with the capture from the southward by the Chesapeake of the capital of "the rebels." This was in accordance with the plan, as we now know, of General Charles Lee, second in command to Washington, while he was a prisoner in New York. He thus proved himself a traitor more despicable even than Arnold. His infamy did not become known until of late years. Moving northward from the head of the Chesapeake Bay, the British encountered Washington at Brandywine and, defeating him, secured an entrance to Philadelphia when it pleased General Howe to enter, which he did on September 26th, amid the welcoming acclaim of the people who remained. The Patriots had generally left the city.

On the 23d the Navy Board ordered all vessels south of Market Street to move down the river and all north to go up the Delaware to escape falling into the hands of the British. Barry's "Effingham" went down the river.

Barry, as the Senior Commander of the Navy at the Port of Philadelphia, had charge of the "row gallies, batteries" and other vessels protecting and maintaining the *chevaux de frize* off Billingsport by sinking obstructions to prevent the passage to the city of any British vessels and thus effectually stopping the channel.

The British erected a battery near the mouth of the Schuylkill upon which Barry's galleys fired at times but seemingly with but little effect, though "playing their part most nobly and acting like men and freemen convincing the world their liberty was merited," to use the words of Thomas McKean to General Rodney.

When, on October 22, 1777, Count Donop attacked the Americans in Fort Mercer at Red Bank, the British fleet coöperated with the land forces, while the Continental vessels under Barry and the Pennsylvania fleet under Hazlewood drove them back, preventing their passage up the river. The British frigate the "Augusta" and the "Merlin" were driven ashore. The "Merlin" was set on fire by its crew. The powder on the "Augusta" exploded and that vessel was blown up. Portions of its remains are in the water off Red Bank to this day.

Fort Mifflin, held by the Americans, was attacked on November 16, 1777. Unable to have the assistance of the Continental or the State Navy, the fort was abandoned. A council of the commanders of the fleet was held, when it was decided that an endeavor should be made at night to take all the vessels up the river, as the British fleet held control of the lower Delaware. To do this it was necessary to pass Philadelphia, then in possession of the British. This was successfully accomplished by the State fleet early in the morning of November 16th. They were "unperceived," says the British account, until the passage had been successfully made. The enemy were more alert the following night when the Continental vessels under Barry endeavored to make the passage. Three or four succeeded. Others had to be burned to prevent capture. The success of this elusive passage up the river emboldened, as we shall see later, Captain Barry, a few months afterwards, to make another successful passage down the river, passing, unmolested, the British vessels off Philadelphia and getting down into the Bay to oppose the British hovering thereabouts.

Barry's operations on the Delaware, while the British occupied Philadelphia, were as brilliant and as audacious in bravery as any services performed during his career. Doubtless from his activity, good judgment and bravery at this period may have proceeded all the successes of his subsequent career. The Continental authorities were made aware at once of the abilities of the gallant man whom they had so early in the struggle for Independence placed in command.

During the attack on Fort Mifflin by the British, Lieutenant Ford, of Barry's "Effingham," and Lieutenant Lyons, of the "Dickinson," deserted. After the British had evacuated Philadelphia these deserters were captured and on September 2, 1778, shot. The execution took place on a guard-boat off Market Street.

After the Continental and State fleets had arrived in the upper Delaware near Bordentown, Washington, in November, 1777, notified the Continental Navy Board there was danger of a British force being sent to destroy the vessels. So he directed they should be sunk. Barry was, by the Board, on November 2d, directed to move the "Effingham" "a little below White Hill" (now Fieldsboro, N.J.) "where she may lie on a soft bottom. You are to sink her there without delay by sunset this evening." But Barry was loath to sink the vessel he had been appointed to command and fight. Later in the month Francis Hopkinson, of the Navy Board, delivered to Captain Barry, as Senior Officer, "orders, in writing," to sink or burn the ships. Captains Barry and Read had taken every measure to defend the vessels which Barry declared he believed would be effectual in repelling any force the enemy would send to destroy them.

Barry and Read protested to the Board against the sinking, saying that if Washington knew the security of the ships he would not order the sinking. Barry offered to go and inform him, but Hopkinson declared Washington had been informed and his order would be carried out. He told Barry that the order should be obeyed; that he would take Washington's opinion in preference to Barry's.

"I told him," related Barry in his defense, when summoned before Congress sitting at York, for disrespect to the Navy Board, "that nevertheless I knew more about a ship than General Washington and the Navy Board together. That I was commissioned by Congress to command the 'Effingham' and, therefore, expected to be consulted before she was destroyed."

The Story of Commodore John Barry

"You shall obey our orders," was the quick and somewhat heated reply. Whereupon Barry left him "of course in high dudgeon," said Barry. "I immediately repaired to my ship, got all clear—and the orders were punctually obeyed"—while Hopkinson himself was on board giving orders which did not permit the vessel to keel and so was "very near upsetting." When Barry reported the condition of the ship to the Navy Board, he was told "it was a misfortune and we must do the best to remedy it," to which Barry replied that nothing would be wanting on his part.

Two attempts to raise the "Effingham" failed for want of men and material, whereupon Mr. Hopkinson said he would raise her himself—"an insult I overlooked, having the getting up of the ship much at heart," Barry told Congress. So he got everything ready and sent for as many of the invalid soldiers as could be had, and with the seamen began to heave. And he too "worked with as much ardor as possible."

"Captain Barry, doth she rise," called Hopkinson.

"No, sir! How can she rise when you keep the people back," replied Barry. This was an allusion to Hopkinson's order that only invalids, well attired, should be sent to assist the seamen.

"Puh! You are always grumbling," retorted Hopkinson.

"What do you say?" quickly cried Barry.

"Go along and mind your own business, you scoundrel," roared Hopkinson.

"It is a lie," said Barry.

"What! Do you tell me I lie?" said Hopkinson.

"It was a lie in them that said so," was Barry's rejoinder.

Hopkinson replied that he would bring Barry to an account for this.

"My answer was," Barry told Congress, "Damn you! I don't value you more than my duty requires."

"Sir! You never minded your duty," retorted Hopkinson.

"I immediately told him he was a liar and that the Continental Congress knew I had minded my duty, and added that had he minded his duty as well the ship would not be in its present condition."

The Navy Board, on December 11, 1777, complained to Congress of the "disrespect and ill treatment which Hopkinson had received from John Barry, commander of the frigate 'Effingham.'"

Barry was summoned to York, Pa., where Congress was in session. On January 10th he attended and made defense, concluding by saying that he considered himself "unworthy the commission of Congress if he tamely put up with treatment other than that due to all Captains of the Navy as gentlemen."

On February 27th the Marine Committee reported to Congress that "Captain Barry ought, within twenty days, make full acknowledgment to the Navy Board of having treated Mr. Hopkinson with indecency and disrespect." Nothing further appears on record, so it is presumed Captain Barry complied and the case closed. At this time Barry was, by order of the same Committee, actively at work destroying British supplies in the lower Delaware from Mantua Creek to Port Penn and Bombay Hook.

Congress was equally divided on a resolution that Captain Barry be not, in consequence of his conduct towards Hopkinson, "employed on the expedition assigned to his conduct by the Marine Committee with the approbation of Congress until the further order of Congress." Had he not been employed, Washington might not, later, have been cheered by the results which Captain Barry achieved in "the expedition" against the British supply vessels coming up the Delaware.

The Story of Commodore John Barry

Washington, amid the desolation of Valley Forge, had his heart torn by the suffering of his Patriot soldiers who bore all, suffered all, hoped all, determined to brave all that their country should be free. From amid that distress Washington sent his thanks for "the good things" Barry sent to the camp.

While the controversy with Hopkinson was being considered and Barry was in the upper Delaware, he projected the plan to attempt the destruction of some of the enemy's vessels lying off Philadelphia by floating down machines in form of ships' buoys filled with powder. These, as they floated past the city, were fired at by the British batteries. This event is known in history as "The Battle of the Kegs."

Singularly, too, Francis Hopkinson, Barry's accuser of want of respect for him made the event memorable by a humorous ditty reflecting upon "British valor displayed."

"The cannons roar from shore to shore,
The small arms make a rattle;
Since war's began, I'm sure no man
E'er saw so strange a battle."

The Loyalists, however, considered the battle as "a most astonishing instance of the activity, bravery and military skill of the Royal Navy of Great Britain. Officers and men exhibited the most unparalleled skill and bravery on the occasion, while the citizens stood as solemn witness of their prowess."

This occurred on Monday, January 5, 1778, a day ever distinguished in history for the memorable "Battle of the Kegs."

CHAPTER VI.

BARRY ATTACKS THE BRITISH SUPPLY SHIPS BELOW PHILADELPHIA—CAPTURES THREE—SENDS SUPPLIES TO WASHINGTON AT VALLEY FORGE—THANKS OF WASHINGTON—WAS BARRY OFFERED A BRITISH COMMAND?

The expedition assigned to Captain Barry which he came near being deprived of by Congress was a cruise in the Delaware River. The Marine Committee, not being directed not to employ Barry, on January 29, 1778, directed him to fit out the pinnace and barges belonging to the frigates for "a cruise in said river under your command." He was empowered to "receive stores and employ such Continental Navy officers and call the number of men necessary for officering, manning, victualing and equipping the boats." He was directed to have frequent occasion to land on each side of the Delaware and to restrain his men from plundering or insulting the inhabitants. The Navy Board was directed to supply "everything necessary for your little fleet" and money to procure supplies. He was directed to inform General Washington of such stores as he might capture which are necessary for the use of the army. He was to sink or destroy the vessels which he could not remove to safety. His "despatch, activity, prudence and valor," were relied on to bring success. If Barry's project to destroy British shipping by explosive machines did not succeed, another form of endeavor dependent more upon skill and bravery would accomplish results as satisfactory as had been hoped for by the floating "score of kegs or more that came floating down the tide."

The Supreme Executive Committee of Pennsylvania, then at Lancaster, on February 7, 1778, notified the Navy Board, then at Burlington, New Jersey, that "a spirit of enterprise to annoy the enemy in the river below Philadelphia had discovered itself in Captain Barry and other officers of the Continental Navy, which promised considerable advantage to the adventurous as well as to the public."

The Story of Commodore John Barry

The Council had waited to find Captain Barry's example inducing the officers and men of the State fleet to engage in the enterprise—of taking all they could get from the enemy, so that any benefit arising from the plan should accrue to those who signalized themselves in the time of danger. So Captain Barry during the night, with four rowboats with twenty-seven men, started from Burlington and succeeded in passing Philadelphia undiscovered and so unmolested by the British. Barry was acting under orders of General Anthony Wayne, a fellow-member of the FRIENDLY SONS OF ST. PATRICK, who sent a detachment from Washington's army to aid in the enterprise. After passing Philadelphia, Barry began the destructive work of destroying forage. On February 26, 1778, he arrived off Port Penn and from there, that day, wrote General Washington at Valley Forge that he had "destroyed the forage from Mantua Creek to this place," amounting to four hundred tons. He would have proceeded further but "a number of the enemy's boats appeared and lined the Jersey shore, depriving us of the opportunity of proceeding on the same purpose." Barry discharged all but four of Washington's men, whom he kept to assist in getting the boats away, as his men were rendered incapable through fatigue.

On March 7, 1778, off Bombay Hook, Barry with twenty-seven men in five rowboats captured the "Mermaid" and the "Kitty," transports from Rhode Island, laden with supplies for the British. He stripped the vessels and sent the supplies northward through New Jersey and burned the vessels. The "Alert," a British schooner with eight four-pounders, twelve four-pound howitzers and thirty-three men properly equipped for an armed vessel, came in sight while Barry was engaged in the encounter with the supply vessels. Barry sent a flag to Captain Morse, of the "Alert," demanding a surrender, promising that the officers would be allowed their private baggage, whereupon the "Alert" was "delivered up" to Captain Barry, who granted parole to the Captain to go to Philadelphia for a fortnight. "The schooner is a most excellent vessel for our purpose," wrote Captain Barry to General Washington two days later, when sending him a "cheese and a jar of pickled oysters" from the store of wines and luxuries intended for General Howe's table. He also sent a plan of New York "which may be of service," which he had taken on the "Alert."

Though a fleet of the enemy's small vessels were in sight, "I am determined," wrote Barry, "to hold the 'Alert' at all events;" that as a number of ships with very little convoy were expected Barry declared that with about forty more men he could give a very good account of them. The next day, March 8, 1778, he reported to the Marine Committee the success of the expedition. On the 11th the Committee congratulated the "gallant commander, brave officers and men concerned in it throughout the whole cruise." He was informed that the "Alert" would be purchased for a cruiser, her name changed to the "Wasp," of which he was to take command or bestow it on some brave, active and prudent officer on a cruise on the coast and off Cape Henlopen, so as "to descry the enemies' vessels coming and going." Barry's "well-known bravery and good conduct" were commended. The British "frigates and small armed vessels," however, attacked Barry. After a long and severe engagement he was obliged to ground and abandon the 'Alert,' though he saved her guns and most of her tackle, so Washington reported to Congress on March 12th.

That day Washington wrote to Barry:

"I have received your favor of the 9th inst. and congratulate you on the success that has crowned your gallantry and address in the late attacks on the enemy's ships. Although circumstances have prevented you from reaping the full benefit of your conquests, yet there is ample consolation in the degree of glory which you have acquired.

"May a suitable recompense always attend your bravery."

Alexander Hamilton, writing to Governor Clinton, of New York, from Washington's Headquarters, Valley Forge, March 12, 1778, said: "We have nothing new in camp save that Captain Barry has destroyed, with a few gunboats, two large ships belonging to the enemy, laden with forage from Rhode Island. He also took an armed schooner which he has since been obliged to run ashore after a gallant defense. 'Tis said he has saved her cannon and stores— among the ordnance four brass howitzers."

Barry with twenty-seven men had captured one major, two captains, three lieutenants, ten soldiers and one hundred seamen and marines—one hundred and sixteen taken by twenty-seven. He captured also many letters and official papers relating to the

Hessians in British service, as well as the Order of *Lion d'Or* for General Knyphausen. This was sent the Hessian general. Barry's success won the admiration of friend and foe. It was at this time Sir William Howe is said to have offered Captain Barry twenty thousand guineas and the command of a British frigate if he would desert the service of the United Colonies. The alleged answer of Barry is stated to have been: "Not the value and command of the whole British fleet can seduce me from the cause of my country."

Any such offer, if made, would more probably have been made by Lord Howe, Commander of the British fleet, brother to General Howe, Commander of the Army. It is of record that he sent Commodore Hazlewood, of the Pennsylvania Navy, a summons to surrender, to which reply was made that he "would not surrender but defend to the last." A like summons to Barry, Commander of the Continental Navy, doubtless received a similar reply, but there is no known evidence or authoritative record that Barry was tempted to desert his country.

WASHINGTON GIVING COMMISSION TO BARRY

CHAPTER VII.

Praise for Barry's Success—British Destroy Barry's "Effingham" and Other Vessels on the Upper Delaware—Appointed to the "Raleigh"—Protects the Coast from North Carolina to Massachusetts—Encounter with Two British Frigates—Barry Runs the "Raleigh" Ashore—His Action Approved and His Bravery Declared.

Barry's operations on the Delaware were of foremost importance at this period of gloom and darkness. The British were in possession of Philadelphia, the Capital of "the rebels." Washington's men were suffering the distress of Valley Forge, ill-fed and scantily clothed. Barry was destroying forage and capturing supplies. General Wayne was operating around Philadelphia, in Pennsylvania, Delaware and New Jersey in a like endeavor.

"For boldness of design and dexterity of execution, Barry's operations were not surpassed, if equaled, during the war," says Frost's *Naval Biography*.

"The gallant action reflects great honor on Captain Barry, his officers and crew," wrote William Ellery, one of Massachusetts' delegates in Congress.

Colonel Laurens wrote his father telling of the deeds of Captain Barry, "to whom great praise is due." Washington reported to Congress "with great pleasure the success" of Captain Barry.

Captain Barry considered the Delaware Bay "the best place for meeting with success where he could use his little squadron." On the upper Delaware where the "Effingham," "Washington" and other Continental vessels had been sunk, near Bordentown, by order of General Washington, in April by his orders, also, the Pennsylvania Navy Board, directed that the galleys, shallops and brigs be dismantled and sunk, shot buried and stores lodged throughout New Jersey. All this after "a rather stubborn insistance on the part of the officers" against so doing, just as Captain Barry had protested. Later in the month Barry's "Effingham," the "Washington" and other Continental vessels were raised "from the soft bottom of the river," but on May 7, 1778, a British force, under Major Maitland, was sent from Philadelphia and burned twenty-one or more vessels and naval stores and destroyed all supplies.

At this time Captain Barry was in command of the squadron in the lower Delaware River and in the Bay. By the destruction of the "Effingham" in the upper Delaware he was without a command other than the temporary one in which he was operating. Accordingly, on May 30, 1778, the Marine Committee appointed him to the command of the frigate "Raleigh," then in Boston Harbor. He was directed to "repair immediately to that place" to take command. He succeeded Captain Thomas Thompson, who was charged with having deserted the "Alfred" (Barry's old-time "Black Prince") in the battle with the British frigates "Ariadne" and "Ceres," by which the "Alfred" became captive.

Captain Barry proceeded to Boston and, taking command of the "Raleigh," refitted her for service and went to sea, stopping at Rhode Island, where he received the orders of Marine Committee, on August 24, 1778, ordering him to cruise in company with the Continental brigantine "Resistance," Captain Burke, between Cape Henlopen and Occracok on the coast of North Carolina to intercept British armed vessels infesting that coast. On May 28th orders were sent to Hampton, Virginia, for delivery to Captain Barry, directing him to take under convoy six or more of the vessels loaded with commissary stores and protect them to the places of destination. Then he and Captain Burke were to proceed and protect the coast line of Virginia and North Carolina, reporting once a week at Hampton for orders, which he, as Senior Officer, should communicate to Captain Burke, and also there receive supplies furnished by the Governor of Virginia.

Captain Barry in the "Raleigh" cruised along the coast from North Carolina to Massachusetts Bay. On September 8, 1778, off Boston Bay he reported to the Marine Committee that many of the guns of the

"Raleigh" had burst in proving and the ship was "exceedingly foul" and unfit to further cruise. He was, on September 28, 1778, directed to proceed to Portsmouth, Virginia, where there was a Continental shipyard, and have the "Raleigh's" bottom cleaned. That done he was to continue "to cruise upon the coast," the "Deane" or any other vessel with him, Barry was to order to cruise while the "Raleigh" was being cleaned.

The Committee had information that the British frigate "Persius," of 32 guns was cruising singly on the coast of South Carolina. Barry was then ordered as soon as his ship was cleaned to extend his cruising ground so as to cover the coast of that State, taking the "Deane" or other vessel with him in search of the "Persius" and endeavor to "take, burn, sink or destroy" the said frigate or any other of the enemy's vessels "that he might fall in with." If he made a capture he was to take it to Charleston and there fit, man her and take her on the cruise with him.

This order, sent to Hampton, Virginia, did not reach the "Raleigh" as, on September 25, 1778, she had sailed from Boston convoying a brigantine and sloop. That day and the following, two British frigates were seen but avoided. The next day—Sunday—the frigates chased the "Raleigh" from nine in the morning until five in the afternoon when, nearing each other, the "Raleigh" hoisted her colors and the headmost frigate "hoisted St. George's ensign." "We gave her a broadside which she returned, tacked and came up on our lee quarter and gave the "Raleigh" a broadside," which carried away its foretopmast and mizzentop gallant mast, which, to "the unspeakable grief" of Captain Barry, caused him, "in a great measure, to lose command" of the "Raleigh," "determined to victory" as he was. "The enemy plied his broadsides briskly, which was returned as brisk," though the "Raleigh" "bore away to prevent the enemy from raking us." The British sheered off and dropped astern. During the night Barry perceived the stern-most ship gaining on us very fast and, being disabled in our sails, masts and rigging and having no possible view of escaping, Captain Barry, with the advice of his officers, ran the "Raleigh" on shore to prevent her falling into the hands of the enemy. The engagement, however, continued "very warm until midnight"—a five-hours' contest, when the frigate sheered off to wait the consort. The "Raleigh's" mizzentopsail had been shot away. Captain Barry ordered the other sails cut loose from the yards. The two frigates appeared and endeavored to cut the "Raleigh" "from the land." The headmost ship proved a two-decker of at least fifty guns. The "Raleigh," "not in the least daunted, received their fire, which was very heavy, and returned ours with redoubled vigor."

"Encouraged by our brave commander, we were determined not to strike," related one of the officers. "After receiving three broadsides from the large ship and the fire of the other frigate on our lee quarter," the "Raleigh" struck the shore, when the enemy poured in two broadsides, which were returned. She then hove in stays, our guns being loaded gave us a good opportunity of raking her, which we did with our whole broadside. After that she bore away and raked us and both British frigates kept up a heavy fire in order to make us strike to them, which we never did. They ceased and came to anchor a mile distant from the "Raleigh."

The island on which the "Raleigh" struck was uninhabited and being rocky could not be fortified for the defense of the ship. The enemy kept up an incessant fire on her and the men being exhausted after the long contest with the two frigates, Captain Barry ordered the men to land and the "Raleigh" to be set on fire. The eighty-five men were landed, but the treachery of Midshipman Jesse Jaycockt, an Englishman, who extinguished the fire, prevented the destruction. The other officers and men were made prisoners before the boats could return to take them off.

This "unequal contest with two ships was fought with great gallantry and though Captain Barry lost his ship he gained laurels for himself and honor for his country. Perhaps no ship was ever better defended," wrote John Brown, Secretary of the Navy Board at Boston to the Marine Committee of Congress, adding, "Captain Barry's conduct is highly approved and his officers and men are greatly pleased with him."

"His good conduct and bravery are universally allowed," said the *Pennsylvania Post*.

Captain Barry "fought with his usual bravery. His officers and men being sworn not to surrender, our brave Captain Barry avoided violating his oath by running the 'Raleigh' ashore," wrote Colonel John Laurens to his father.

The British frigates were the "Experiment," of 50 guns, and the "Unicorn," of 22 guns, or 72 guns against Barry's 32. The latter had ten men killed and was greatly damaged in hull and rigging in the contest of nine hours duration. The "Raleigh" lost twenty-five killed and wounded. The ship was added to the Royal Navy under the same name. This battle took place off Seal Island, or Fox Island, in Penobscot Bay.

Cooper's *History of the Navy* said, "Captain Barry gained credit for his gallantry on this occasion."

"A noble and daring defence," said Watson's *Annals of Philadelphia*.

This disaster left Barry without a ship. The loss, though regrettable, did not lessen his reputation as a skillful and sagacious commander nor mar the character he had won for bravery.

The Marine Committee in ordering the Navy Board at Boston to "order a Court of Inquiry on Captain Barry's conduct," said: "The loss of the 'Raleigh' is certainly a very great misfortune, but we have a consolation in reflecting that the spirited and gallant behavior of her commander has done honor to our flag."

And that it held him not censurable is shown by its statement that as "Captain Harding has been appointed to the command of the frigate at Norwich named the 'Confederacy,' which prevents our giving that ship to Captain Barry."

The Committee was ready at once to give him another command had a vessel been ready for him. That too without waiting the action of the Court of Inquiry, which it had ordered. But the Committee had soon occasion to give an appointment which showed the estimation in which his abilities were held as the foremost naval commander, worthy to be entrusted with its best commands and ships.

ORDER TO CAPTAIN BARRY

CHAPTER VIII.

Barry Appointed to Command an Expedition Against Florida—Expedition Abandoned, Barry Enters the Pennsylvania Privateer Service—Makes Captures—Resists the Imprisonment of His Crew—"My Name is John Barry."

That the loss of the "Raleigh" brought no discredit upon Captain Barry, but rather added to his reputation as a brave and skillful commander is attested by the action of the Marine Committee in appointing him to command an expedition against East Florida.

Major-General Lincoln was to command the Continental and State army forces in the reduction of St. Augustine, Florida, as it "was of the highest importance to the United States."

On November 10, 1778, Congress Resolved:

"That Captain John Barry be and is hereby directed to take command of all armed vessels employed in the intended expedition, subject to the order of the Commander-in-Chief in the Southern Department; and that this commission continue in force till the expedition of the intended invasion of the Province of East Florida or till the further order of Congress; that he proceed with the utmost despatch to the State of Maryland in order to expedite the equipment of the gallies to be furnished by that State and proceed with them to Charleston in South Carolina."

At Charleston armed gallies from Virginia were to be joined. "The success of the expedition depended in the most essential manner on their service." The Continental share of all property taken would be released to the captors.

To prevent difference among officers of the respective States whose gallies would be employed, Captain John Barry was appointed to command the naval part of the expedition. Captain Barry "made some extraordinary demands upon Congress for allowance of a table and a secretary, which the House did not determine on," wrote Henry Laurens, President of Congress, to General Lincoln; adding that "though Captain Barry is a brave and active seaman, the intended service is not pleasing to him, 'tis possible, therefore, he may wish to avoid it and besides you will find old commanders in the two Southern States who will be much mortified should he actually proceed and take the command of them, consequences will arise which will be disagreeable to you and which may prove detrimental to the service."

The British probably became aware of the intended invasion and so organized a counter-movement against General Lincoln and obliged him to defend his occupancy of Charleston. General Clinton, on December 26, 1778, sailed from New York and a month later, delayed by storms, reached Savannah, the base of his operations against Lincoln. This obliged Congress to abandon its projected expedition against East Florida. So Captain Barry's "extraordinary demands" or the jealousies of the Southern naval officers were, by the course of events, set aside. The aggressive movement of Sir Henry Clinton had frustrated the intended invasion and so all the minor considerations involved therein.

But the high esteem in which Barry was held was proven by the appointment to command the expedition and this, too, immediately after the loss of the "Raleigh." His defense of the "Raleigh" was so bravely performed that the appointment to the Southern expedition was given him as the best testimonial of worth and of fidelity to duty. The loss of the "Raleigh" and the abandonment of the invasion of East Florida left Captain John Barry without an available Continental ship. But such a brave and active seaman could not be listless nor idle while an opportunity could be found or made for doing service for his country. When the "Effingham" and other vessels were tied up in the Delaware, Captain Barry became a landsman and did shore duty, leading a company of volunteers in the Trenton and Princeton campaign.

The Story of Commodore John Barry

Now that his country had no ship to give him to do duty for America, he entered the service of his adopted State, Pennsylvania, and became "a bold privateer" by becoming commander of the Letter-of-Marque, the brig "Delaware," owned by Irwin & Co., of Philadelphia. His commission bears date of February 15, 1779. It is in the Lenox Library, New York.

The "Delaware" was a new brig of 200 tons, built to replace the schooner of the same name, which had been driven on the New Jersey shore and set on fire to escape the British early on the morning of November 21, 1777, when the State's Navy had passed up the Delaware River after the attack on Fort Mifflin.

The new "Delaware" carried ten guns and forty-five men when commissioned, but Captain Barry increased the force to twelve guns and sixty men.

The day he was commissioned he stood sponsor and his wife a witness to the baptism of Anna, daughter of Thomas, his brother, born on that morning. On July 21st following, Captain Barry's wife, Sarah Austin Barry, became a Catholic and was baptised, conditionally, Anna Barry, wife of Thomas, being the only sponsor. At this time Captain Barry was cruising in the West Indies. Judith, "the slave of Captain John Barry," an adult, was also baptised on August 19, 1779.

In the "Delaware" Captain Barry made two cruises to Port-au-Prince. Of his first voyage no record has been discovered, but of his second there is sufficient in the account given by his Mate, John Kessler. The "Delaware" sailed on its second cruise in the fall of 1779 in company with three other Letter-of-Marque brigs and one schooner. Of this fleet Captain Barry was made Commodore. He was always so appointed whenever two or more vessels were assigned to one cruise or expedition in which he engaged. When abreast of Cape Henlopen the British sloop-of-war the "Harlem," with eighty-five men and fourteen four-pounders, was taken without resistance, though the officers escaped in boats after heaving overboard all the guns.

The Story of Commodore John Barry

The "Harlem" was sent to Philadelphia. The crew was delivered to the militia at Chincopague. Captain Barry reported to the owners that "the commanders in our little fleet are very complaisant and obliging to each other." That the "Harlem" had fourteen four-pounders and eighty-five men. The guns and other things were thrown overboard without firing a shot. The Captain, with ten men, went off in a whale-boat, "but," reported Captain Barry, "we have reason to think, is since overset." The prisoners were taken out, a prize crew put on board, the "Harlem" sent to Philadelphia and the men landed at Sinipaxan, Virginia, as they were too many to keep with safety on board the little fleet. "We have every reason in the world to think we shall catch more before long," reported Barry. The "Harlem" was "a fine vessel and had been a cruiser since the enemy took New York, but at present she is much out of tune," he added.

Of the rest of the voyage out and home nothing specially noteworthy occurred except that a merchant ship from Liverpool was captured and later retaken by the noted Goodrich and carried into Bermuda.

During the war there was often contention between the commanders of the Continental and those of the States' service. The Continentals, when in need of men, often impressed the seamen of the States' fleet and also those of merchant vessels. On Captain Barry's return to the Delaware River the Continental frigate "Confederacy" lay at Chester. She had been impressing the crews of merchant vessels coming up the river. The pilot gave this information to the crew of the "Delaware." It alarmed them very much and many desired to be put on shore. Captain Barry addressed them saying, "My lads, if you have the spirit of freemen you will not desire to go ashore nor tamely submit against your wills to be taken away, although all the force of all the frigate's boats' crew were to attempt to exercise such a species of tyranny." This address, records Kessler, satisfied them, as it implied his consent to their defending themselves. They resolved to do it at all hazards, and for that purpose put themselves under the command and direction of the boatswain and armed themselves with muskets, pistols and boarding pikes, and thus arrived within hailing distance of the "Confederacy." Her commander ordered the brig's maintopsail to be hove to the mast. Captain Barry answered that he could not without getting his vessel ashore. The commander of the frigate then ordered that the brig should come to anchor.

Captain Barry gave no answer but continued on his way, beating up with tide and flood and wind, when a gun was fired from the frigate and a boat, manned, left her and came towards the "Delaware." Captain Barry directed that the officers of the boat should be admitted on board, but as to the men with them, the "Delaware's" crew could do as they pleased. The boat soon arrived and two officers, armed, jumped on board and on the quarterdeck, ordering the maintopsail halyards to be cast off, which, however, was not done. Captain Barry asked whether they were sent to take command of his vessel. The boat's crew were about coming on board when the "Delaware's" men threatened instant death to all who came on board.

The officers after trying to intimidate our boatswain by presenting their pistols at him, and finding it of no avail, hastily sprang into their boats and left.

Another gun was fired from the "Confederacy." Captain Barry ordered the guns cleared and declared that if a rope-yard was injured he would give the "Confederacy" a whole broadside. A third gun was fired. Captain Barry hailed and asked the name of the commander of the frigate.

The answer was "Lieutenant Gregory."

Captain Barry addressed him: "Lieutenant Gregory, I advise you to desist from firing. This is the brig 'Delaware,' belonging to Philadelphia and my name is John Barry."

"Nothing further was said or done by Lieutenant Gregory," recorded Mate Kessler, who added: "Our whole crew arrived at Philadelphia, but the other vessels of our fleet were obliged to anchor, as the pressing of those who did not get on shore obliged them to remain until assistance was sent from Philadelphia. After our arrival Barry left the command of the brig, he having been ordered to take charge of a Continental 74-gun ship then building in the State of New Hampshire," relates Kessler. James Collins, First Lieutenant, became Captain Barry's successor in command of the "Delaware," which had taken two prizes, the distribution of which was made among the officers and crew, Kessler receiving "in the threefold capacity of clerk, steward and captain of marines."

CHAPTER IX.

CAPTAIN BARRY APPOINTED TO SUPERINTEND THE BUILDING OF THE "AMERICA," FRIGATE—GIVEN COMMAND OF THE "ALLIANCE" AS SUCCESSOR OF LANDAIS, THE FRENCHMAN—THE DISCOVERY OF ARNOLD'S TREASON—"WHOM CAN WE TRUST NOW?"—THE ANSWER TO ARNOLD.

The Continental 74 to which Captain Barry was sent immediately on his arrival at Philadelphia in the "Delaware" was the frigate "America," then building at Portsmouth, New Hampshire. To this command he was appointed on November 6, 1779, by the Marine Committee of Congress, which that day notified the Navy Board at Boston that Captain Barry on his way to Portsmouth, New Hampshire, where he goes to hasten the building and fitting out of the new ship on the stocks at that place, would present the notification desiring the Committee to "push forward with all possible expedition" the work Captain Barry had been entrusted with. Barry's orders were "to hasten as much as may be in your power the completing of that ship, which we are desirous of having done with all despatch."

On November 20th, as desired by Captain Barry, Captain George Jerry Osborne was appointed to command the marines of the ship, but as it would be "a considerable time before there is occasion to raise the men," he was appointed "on the principle of his being useful in doing matters relative to the ship until that time." How long Captain Barry continued to superintend the building of the new Continental ship—later named the "America," does not appear, but on June 1, 1780, there is record in the *Pennsylvania Archives* [Vol. I, 5th Series] that Captain John Barry became the commander of the Pennsylvania privateer, the "American," of 14 guns and 70 men. Possibly the work of directing the construction of a vessel was not congenial to the active spirit of one who was at his best amid the more earnest exertions required by a life at sea, seeking the destruction or capture of the armed vessels of the enemy. So again he

The Story of Commodore John Barry

became a privateersman in the service of his State. He so served three months.

On June 26, 1781, Captain John Paul Jones was appointed, in succession to Barry, to superintend the construction of the "America," while Barry was doing service at sea in command of the "Alliance." The expense of launching and equipping the "America" was paid from the shares of the United States "in the prizes taken by Captain Barry" in the first cruise of the "Alliance" under his command. The Board of Admiralty were directed to assign these shares to Robert Morris by Resolution of Congress, June 3, 1781. The "America" when launched in November, 1781, was presented to France to replace the "Magnifique," wrecked in Boston Harbor.

The Continental Marine Committee, knowing well Barry's worth, on September 5, 1780, appointed him "to the command of the Continental frigate 'Alliance' now in the port of Boston." He was "directed to repair there as soon as possible to get the ship ready for sea with all possible despatch." The "Alliance" was the largest and finest vessel of the Continental Navy.

Thus we see again that the best available position was always given to Captain Barry. The first armed cruiser under direct Continental authority—the "Lexington"—was given him, then the "Effingham," of 32 guns, the largest armament of any vessel, was assigned him, and he was made Senior Commander of the Port of Philadelphia. On its destruction by the British, while he was operating in the lower Delaware, he was appointed to the "Raleigh." On its loss, for which Captain Barry suffered no detriment, he was made commander of the projected expedition to Florida. When that enterprise was abandoned he was given command of a fleet of the Navy of Pennsylvania. At the termination of the cruise the appointment to construct the best vessel the country had projected was given him. Then he was commissioned to the "Alliance," the best and finest vessel the United Colonies ever possessed. In that he remained as commander while the war continued, and at its close he was Commodore of all armed vessels remaining in the service of the Colonies, just as Washington was Commander-in-Chief of all the forces, military and naval, at the end of the war. As commander of the fleet, Barry was second to Washington.

The "Alliance," which Captain Barry took charge of in September, 1780, was so named in honor of the alliance with France. As a further compliment to the French, Captain Pierre Landais, a Frenchman, had been appointed Captain. He was relieved of the command and Captain Barry succeeded him. These were the only commanders the "Alliance" ever had—Landais the Frenchman and Barry the Irishman. Landais is buried in St. Patrick's cemetery, New York; Barry in St. Mary's, Philadelphia. One in faith and one in endeavor for our country.

The "Alliance" was the only American vessel in the expedition sent out by King Louis XVI, under John Paul Jones, which resulted in the ever memorable encounter with, and capture of, the "Serapis" by the "Bonne Homme Richard," commanded by Captain John Paul Jones. During the battle the "Alliance" twice fired into Jones' vessel and did damage. For this, on arrival in France, he was called on to make explanations and John Paul Jones, as Commodore of all American vessels in Europe, was appointed by Commissioner Benjamin Franklin, on June 16, 1780, to take "command of the 'Alliance' in her present intended voyage to America." But Silas Deane supported Landais, who ordered Jones off the vessel and set sail for America. On the voyage, his mental faculties becoming more erratic, the officers took the command from him and entrusted it to Lieutenant James Degges.

On arrival at Boston, Captain Barry was appointed to the command and the Courts of Inquiry and Courts-Martial tried Landais and dismissed him from the service. He died in New York in 1818 and is buried in St. Patrick's graveyard.

Captain Barry now commanded "the most perfect piece of naval architecture" than which the navies of France or England had none more complete. Landais and Barry were the only duly commissioned and regularly appointed by Continental authority commanders of the "Alliance," who at sea, on voyage or in battle ever directed her operations, yet a block of timber of the "Alliance" exhibited in the Revolutionary Relic Museum at Independence Hall is inscribed: "Commanded by John Paul Jones during the Revolutionary War."

There is no mention of its chief commander, John Barry, and that ignoring of his right to recognition is within sight of his statue erected by THE FRIENDLY SONS OF ST. PATRICK, of Philadelphia, March 16, 1907. Let that Society now secure the Commodore's right to the command his country gave him.

The appointment of Captain Barry had special significance at the time it was made—after the discovery of the treason of Benedict Arnold. He had issued on October 7, 1780, an "Address to the Soldiers of the American Army," in which he declared he thought "it infinitely wiser and safer to cast his confidence upon Great Britain's justice and generosity than to trust a monarchy too feeble to establish your Independence, so perilous to her distant dominions and the enemy of the Protestant faith."

Washington, in almost faint-hearted despair on the discovery of Arnold's treachery, had asked: "Whom can we trust now?" Was the answer to Washington and Arnold that made by the Marine Committee of the Continental Congress by the appointment of Captain John Barry to the largest, finest and best American war-vessel named in honor of an alliance with France, the alleged "enemy of the Protestant faith," as Arnold had declared?

Was that the answer to Arnold by the Congress whom he had denounced "as mean and profligate" and "praying a soul out of purgatory," because the members had attended the Requiem service in St. Mary's Church, Philadelphia, in behalf of the soul of Don Juan de Miralles, the Spanish Agent to the Congress, and in the very church which Captain Barry attended when in Philadelphia.

The Irish-born Catholic, John Barry, could be trusted with the very best when the native-born Protestant, Arnold, had betrayed the country for pelf and position among the oppressors of the native land of John Barry and the native land of the infamous Benedict Arnold.

What more could the adopted land of John Barry do for one who had been so faithful and so helpful from the first day of opportunity to serve her? It will erect a monument at the Capital of the Nation for America as Ireland's SONS OF ST. PATRICK have erected one at Independence Hall. His new country had given him the first, and at all times the best, she had to bestow, as his native land had given to America. Place of birth nor creed of faith made no disparagement of such superior worth as John Barry possessed.

The Congress that had, to the people of Great Britain, denounced Barry's religion as "one fraught with impiety, bloodshed, rapine and murder in every part of the globe," had given to the Irish-born Catholic who gave the best he possessed in talent, ability and service to the cause of America, had also given him the first of her war vessels, continued to give him the best she, too, possessed and, finally, while the native-born traitor almost paralyzed the hearts of the patriots, gave to the foreign-born and staunch Catholic, the foremost vessel in her navy, one "so swift, so warlike, stout and strong," as to be the admiration of Europe's most expert naval commanders, while America had dismissed from her service, as incompetent, the native-born Esek Hopkins, the first Commander-in-Chief of the Navy of the Colony. It is somewhat singular, therefore, that the foremost naval commanders of the Navy during the Revolutionary War were John Barry, of Ireland, and John Paul Jones, of Scotland—"foreigners," as John Adams spoke of both in 1813.

The lines of the Poet of the Revolution, Philip Freneau, may most appropriately be inserted here, to show the regard in which the vessel was held while John Barry was its commander:

"When she unfurls her flowing sails,
Undaunted by the fiercest gales,
In dreadful pomp she plows the main,
While adverse tempests rage in vain.
When she displays her gloomy tier,

The Story of Commodore John Barry

The boldest Britons freeze with fear,
And, owning her superior might,
Seek their best safety in their flight.
But when she pours the dreadful blaze
And thunder from her cannon plays,
The bursting flash that wings the ball,
Compels those foes to strike or fall."

"She was in many engagements and always victorious—a fortunate ship—a remarkably fast sailer—could always choose her combat—could either fight or run away—always beating her adversary by fight or flight," Philadelphia's annalist, Watson, made that record of her.

Such was the vessel commanded by Captain John Barry, the Wexford boy, in the closing and eventful year of the Revolution, which established our country's Independence and Liberty, to become the home of countless thousands of all lands who might enjoy the Liberties John Barry had so conspicuously aided in winning.

CHAPTER X.

The "Alliance" Sails for France—Captures a British Cruiser—Return to America—The Loss of the "La Fayette"—Mutiny.

The selection of John Barry, at this crisis in our country's struggle for Liberty and Independence, to the command of the foremost ship of the new Republic is a most conspicuous and honorable testimony to his merits, abilities and services. None additional is needed.

The "Alliance" was selected to convey Colonel John Laurens as a special Commissioner to France to seek "an immediate, ample and efficacious succor in money, large enough to be a foundation for substantial arrangement of finance, to revive public credit and give vigor to future operations."

There was delay in sailing owing to a shortness of crew and the inability to procure recruits. In the meantime Captain Barry was, on November 10, 1780, appointed, by the Navy Board of the Eastern Department, President of a Court-Martial, together with Captains Hoystead Hucker, Samuel Nicholson and Henry Johnson, Lieutenants Silas Devol, Patrick Fletcher, Nicholas E. Gardner and Samuel Pritchard, Lieutenant of Marine, to meet on November 21st to try Lieutenant James Degges to determine whether he was justified in revolting against the authority of Captain Landais of the "Alliance" and usurping command on the voyage from France. A Court-Martial was also held for the trial of Captain Landais, and he was dismissed the service. There is much interesting history connected with these trials, but they do not properly enter into this recital further than to say that Captain Landais' erratic conduct in command of the "Alliance" was due to mental deficiencies as was afterwards generally acknowledged. These became so manifest in the voyage to America that the officers took the command from him.

On February 2, 1781, so impatient at the delay had become Colonel Laurens that, as all other resources had failed, he applied to General

The Story of Commodore John Barry

Benjamin Lincoln to allow recruits for the army fitted for marine service to be engaged and nowhere so advantageously employed.

Patrick Sheridan, an enlisted soldier of Boston, is one known to have been given leave to join the "Alliance." On February 11, 1781, the "Alliance" sailed from Boston with Colonel Laurens, Thomas Paine, Comte de Noailles, brother-in-law of Lafayette and other celebrities. On the way to France the "Alliance" captured, on March 4th, the British cruiser "Alert," which had possession of the "La Buonia Compagnia," a Venetian ship which, "contrary to the Laws of Nations and every principle of justice" had been seized by the British cruiser called the "Alert" from Glasgow, Francis Russell commander, by whom the Venetian crew were put in irons and otherwise cruelly treated.

Captain Barry released the Venetian "out of respect for the Laws of Nations and the rights of neutrality." Colonel Laurens in reporting to Congress, from L'Orient, March 11, 1781, where the "Alliance" had arrived two days before, related the action of Captain Barry, whereupon on June 26th it was resolved that Congress approve of Captain Barry's conduct in releasing the ship belonging to the Republic of Venice, retaken by him from a British privateer on March 4th last, it being the determination always to pay the utmost respect to the rights of neutral commerce. The Venetian Senate also expressed to Franklin, our Ambassador at Paris, through the Ambassador of Venice, their "grateful sense of the friendly behavior of Captain Barry, commander of the 'Alliance,' in rescuing one of the ships of their State from an English privateer and setting her at liberty."

It may be remarked as a singular circumstance that the "Alert" was, probably, the cruiser which, on September 10, 1777, had captured Barry's first command, the "Lexington," which was then commanded by Captain Henry Johnson and which Barry had, in March, 1778, captured in the Delaware Bay, but which was retaken by the British a few days later and which, on September 17, 1778, captured the American cruiser "La Fayette." If so, Captain Barry's gratification must have been great in again capturing the "Alert."

The Story of Commodore John Barry

The importance of Captain Barry's services in this voyage must be noted. He succeeded in conveying to France Colonel Laurens, whose father had been sent on a similar mission, but had been taken prisoner while on the way, and at the time of his son's going on the same mission was a prisoner in the Tower at London. Captain Barry's responsibility was, therefore, great. Skill and acuteness were most essential to avoid encounter with a superior British force and thus endanger the safety of the special Commissioner charged with so important a duty at this "infinitely critical posture of our affairs," as Washington wrote Franklin.

To promptly and safely convey Colonel Laurens was more important to the general good than for Barry to make captures and prizes. Yet he not only performed the duty assigned him, but took two prizes from the enemy—its "Alert" and its own prize, the Venetian ship, restoring it to its country.

Barry's captures were, in notable cases, double captives, taking two in each encounter. On the Delaware Bay expedition he had taken the "Mermaid" and the "Kitty," which he held and the "Alert" which was retaken. Now we find him taking that "Alert" and its prize. These double captures we shall, later, see repeated—taking two prizes in one battle—killing two birds with one stone, as it were. And it took two British cruisers to inflict the only loss he ever had—the loss of the "Raleigh."

Captain Barry took the "Alert" to L'Orient, where the crew were imprisoned. Laurens secured from France a gift of six millions from the King—as well as clothing and military stores. It was sent in the "Resolute" which sailed from Brest, June 1, 1781, and arrived at Boston August 25th. It was this money which moved Washington's army to Yorktown, Virginia, by paying the army one month's pay in specie and enabling supplies to be furnished. Congress had no credit to get money or supplies until the arrival of the French funds. Other portions of the money were used to pay overdue French loans. That was our hard-pressed country's method of paying its debts.

The Story of Commodore John Barry

The importance of the duty assigned Captain Barry to get Colonel Laurens to France is thus made manifest. Well performed, its results brought the downfall of British supremacy in America. Failure to safely convey Laurens would have brought untold disaster upon the cause of Independence and Liberty and, mayhap, long have delayed the winning and the triumph.

On March 23, 1781, Captain Barry, after obtaining supplies needed, was assigned the Letter-of-Marque vessel "Marquis de La Fayette," commanded by Captain Gallatheau, which was loaded with stores for Congress, and directed that, as he was about to return to America, that the "La Fayette" would proceed under his convoy to Philadelphia. On March 29th the "Alliance" and "La Fayette" sailed from L'Orient in company.

When the "Alliance" left L'Orient on her returning cruise to America, Captain Barry, by orders of Franklin, directed Captain Gallatheau, of the ship "Marquis La Fayette," to proceed to the United States under convoy of the "Alliance," as the vessel was laden with one hundred tons of saltpetre, twenty-six iron eighteen-pounders, fifteen thousand gunbarrels, leather, uniforms for ten thousand men and cloth for five or six thousand. After being under convoy for three weeks in a gale of wind which split the sails of the "Alliance," the "La Fayette" disappeared. Captain Barry gave signals by flags and guns and cruised about for two days in search of the missing vessel. Five days after the separation the "Suffolk," British man-of-war, of 74 guns, met the "La Fayette" and after three hours' battle made her captive though reduced to "a perfect hulk." For thirteen days she was towed by the "Suffolk."

Investigation made by Congress into the cause of this great loss showed, by the evidence of Captain Robeson, on board the "La Fayette," that the separation was the fault of Captain Gallatheau by sailing away from the "Alliance" contrary to every argument of Captain Robeson. The loss aggregated four hundred and fifty tons of public stores and two hundred men, besides the armament of twenty-six eighteen-pound guns and fourteen six-pounders.

The Story of Commodore John Barry

On March 30th a mutiny plot was discovered among the crew of the "Alliance." It is best related in the words of Kessler, Barry's friend and officer:

"An Indian, one of the forecastle men, gave Captain Barry information of a combination among the crew for the purpose of taking the ship, and pointed out three who had striven to prevail on him to be concerned therein. The three men were immediately put in irons and all the officers, with such of the crew as could be confided in, were armed and required to remain all night on deck. On the next morning all hands were called and placed on the forecastle, booms and gangways, excepting the officers and such part of the crew in whom Captain Barry confided, who, armed strongly, guarded the quarterdeck, the steerage and the main deck to keep the remainder of the crew together on the forecastle and boom. The three designated men were brought out of their irons on the quarterdeck, and being stripped and hoisted by the thumbs to the mizzen-stay, underwent a very severe whipping before either would make any confession. As their accomplices were disclosed they were called to the quarterdeck, stripped and tied to the ridge-rope of the netting and the whipping continued until it was thought all was disclosed that could possibly be obtained, which proved to be: that it was intended to take the ship on her passage out by killing all the officers in the middle of the watch of the night, except Lieutenant Patrick Fletcher who was to navigate her to some port in Ireland, or, on failure, to be destroyed. A quartermaster, one of the mutineers, was to have command. They all had been bound by an oath on the Bible, administered by the Captain's assistant cabin steward, and had also signed their names in a round-robin, so-called, but that they found no opportunity on the outward passage and intended to accomplish taking of the ship as aforesaid immediately on leaving France. But on coming out of L'Orient we lost a man overboard who was one of the chief ring-leaders, and they, considering that as a bad omen, threw the round-robin overboard and relinquished their designs. The three principals were placed securely in irons and the remainder, after being admonished by Captain Barry, and on their solemn declaration to conduct themselves well, were permitted to return to ship's duty. This mutiny was discovered Sunday, March 31, 1781."

The Story of Commodore John Barry

On April 2d two British armed cruisers were seen at seven in the morning. The "Alliance" gave chase and the two Britishers "stood for" the "Alliance." They neared each other at ten o'clock when the two gave the "Alliance" a broadside, which was "returned doublefold" so effectively that one struck her flag and hove to. She was the "Mars," of twenty twelve-pounders, two sixes and twelve fourpounders and one hundred and eleven men. The other ran while the "Alliance" "fired a number of bow chasers at her" and in an hour hove to and surrendered. She was the "Minerva," mounting eight four-pounders and fifty-five men. The "Alliance" received "considerable damage" from the shot of the enemy. Lieutenant Fletcher and fourteen men were placed in charge of the "Minerva" as a prize crew. Here again in one battle Captain Barry captures two of the enemy's cruisers. The "Alliance" continued the cruise and went to the West India waters seeking prizes.

On May 2d a brig and a snow (a small vessel) loaded with sugar from Jamaica for London were captured and being manned from the "Alliance" was ordered to Boston. Again two captures. Later in the day a fleet of sixty-five sail, convoyed by ten sail of line, were observed but prudently not molested by Captain Barry. Later in the day a brig from Jamaica bound to Bristol, England. We "gave the brig two bow guns at meridian," notes the log of the "Alliance." She surrendered. "Sent our boats, on board and took the prisoners out." The next day another vessel, with seven four-pounders also from Jamaica to Bristol, was taken and the prisoners brought on board the "Alliance."

Not until May 28th was there another opportunity found, when early on that morning an armed ship and a brig were discovered about a league distant. At sunrise they hoisted the English colors and beat drums. At the same time Captain Barry displayed the American colors. By eleven o'clock Captain Barry hailed the ship and was answered that she was the "Atalanta" ship-of-war belonging to His Britannic Majesty, commanded by Captain Sampson Edwards. Captain Barry then told Captain Edwards that he, John Barry, commanded the Continental frigate the "Alliance" and advised him to haul down the English colors.

Captain Edwards replied, "Thank you, Sir. Perhaps I may after a trial."

The firing then began. The "Alliance" had not wind enough for steerage way. The enemy being lighter vessels, by using sweeps, got and kept athwart the stern of the "Alliance" so that she could not bring half her guns to bear upon them, and often but one gun out astern to bear on the two—thus lying like a log the greater part of the time. Captain Barry received a wound in the shoulder from a grape shot. He remained on the quarterdeck until exhausted by loss of blood, when he was helped to the cock-pit for treatment. Soon the colors of the "Alliance" were shot away. This caused the enemy to believe the Americans had struck their colors. They gave three cheers and manned their shrouds expecting a surrender. But the colors of the "Alliance" were again run up—a breeze sprung up—a broadside was given the "Atalanta" and another given the "Trepassy," the brig. They then struck their colors to the "Alliance." Captain Smith, of the "Trepassy," was killed. The Captain of the "Atalanta" was brought on board and taken to Captain Barry, wounded in his cabin. Captain Edwards advanced and presented his sword. Captain Barry received it but at once returned it, saying:

"I return it to you, Sir. You have merited it. Your King ought to give you a better ship. Here is my cabin at your service. Use it as your own."

He then ordered Lieutenant King, of the "Trepassy" brig to be brought to him. The crew of the "Atalanta" and the prisoners Barry had on the "Alliance," numbering 250, should all be put on the "Trepassy," her cannon thrown overboard, and she sent to Halifax as a cartel for the exchange of American prisoners, while the Captain and Lieutenant remained as hostages. The "Atalanta" was retaken by the "Charlestown" and "Vulture." On account of Captain Barry's wound, the "Alliance" made all sail for Boston. Kessler relates that when Captain Barry had been carried to his cabin to have his wounds dressed, the Lieutenant later went to him and reporting that the "Alliance" was very much damaged, many men killed and

The Story of Commodore John Barry

wounded and of the disadvantages for want of wind, asked "Shall the colors be struck?"

Captain Barry passionately answered: "No, Sir, and if the ship cannot be fought without me, I will be brought on deck." The officer immediately returned to deck. Captain Barry, after being dressed in haste, was on his way to the deck when the enemy struck. The "Alliance" lost eleven killed and twenty-four wounded. From her crew of two hundred and eighty—three prize crews had been taken—fifty were on the sick list. A few of these were able to sit between decks and hand powder to the magazine. There were more than one hundred prisoners on board, as well as those of the crew of a mutinous disposition. Add to all this disadvantage the total calm prevailing until near the end of the contest, the capture of the two British vessels was one of special noteworthy importance. "It was considered a most brilliant exploit and an unequivocal evidence of the unconquerable firmness and intrepidity of the victor," says Frost's *Naval Biography*. Here again we find Captain Barry adding to his record of capturing two prizes in one action.

The "Alliance" continued cruising, searching for other prey, but not meeting any, made for Boston, where she arrived June 6, 1781. Captain Barry's wound was yet in a dangerous condition. So he sent Kessler to Philadelphia to bring on Mrs. Barry. The "Alliance" being much shattered in her masts, sails and rigging, a thorough overhauling and repairing was needed. The three mutineers were tried and condemned to be hanged. The sentence was commuted to "serve during the war." Captain Barry refused their admission on the "Alliance," so they were delivered to a recruiting party as soldiers.

CHAPTER XI.

JOHN PAUL JONES SEEKS TO BE "HEAD OF THE NAVY" IN PLACE OF BARRY—BARRY TAKES LAFAYETTE TO FRANCE, AFTER THE SURRENDER OF CORNWALLIS, ON "BUSINESS OF THE UTMOST IMPORTANCE"—ORDERED TO TAKE NO PRIZES—LANDS LAFAYETTE—RETURNS TO AMERICA.

On July 25, 1781, Captain Barry reported to the Board of Admiralty that he was "almost recovered" of his wound and in a few days would be able for duty, his presence being very requisite on account of the scarcity of officers. He made recommendations for places. On June 24th Captain James Nicholson had written Captain Barry congratulating him upon his success. He related in detail the endeavors of Captain John Paul Jones by personal application to members of Congress to have himself declared "Head of the Navy." He told Barry that his "arrival and success came opportunely and I did not fail to make use of it in presence of Captain Jones and some of his advocate members by observing that you had acquitted yourself well, which they acknowledged. I then told them they could not do less than make you an Admiral also. I had not a sentence in reply. It irritated Jones so much that he was obliged to decamp." This shows that among naval men Barry was then regarded as "Head of the Navy"—as he was in fact if not by title.

In 1781 the Admiralty and Navy Boards were abolished by Congress and all naval affairs given to the Finance Department, supervised by Robert Morris. At this time the "Alliance" and the "Deane," frigates, constituted the whole of the effective navy. On September 21st Mr. Morris notified Captain Barry that it was projected to have the two frigates sent out upon a cruise under Barry's command to "disturb the enemy" by taking prizes, and neither fixing the cruising ground nor its length of time, knowing Barry would take "the most likely course and be anxious to meet such events as will do honor to the American flag and promote the general interest." He was to transmit at every opportunity reports of his operations to Morris and to General Washington any intelligence which may affect his operations. But, late in October, the "Deane" not being manned as soon as the "Alliance," Barry was directed to proceed to sea as soon as the "Alliance" would be ready. But the victory at Yorktown on October 19th, when Cornwallis surrendered his army to the combined French and American forces and to the French fleet, caused a change to be made in the movements of the "Alliance."

Instead of going out to seek prizes to procure funds to be applied to the support of the small navy, Captain Barry, on November 21, 1781, was directed to take Lafayette to France "on business of the utmost importance to America." So urgent was this mission that Barry was directed to take part of the crew of the "Deane," place them on the "Alliance" and to take such French seamen as the Consul could procure. If still short of men the Governor of Massachusetts should be applied to for permission to impress seamen wherever found. Besides Lafayette, his brother-in-law, Vicomte de Noailles, General Du Portail, Colonel Gouvion, Major La Combe and others were also taken on the "Alliance."

Morris directed that "the safe and speedy arrival of Marquis Lafayette is of such importance that I think it most consistent with my duty to restrain you from cruising on the passage. You are, therefore, to avoid all vessels and keep in mind as your sole object to make a quiet and safe passage to some port in France."

Regarding stores for the accommodation of the French gentlemen, "Let it be done with discretion; remember we are not rich enough to be extravagant nor so poor as to act meanly." If funds were needed for a return cruise Barry was advised to "prevail with the Marquis to give you credit, but you must remember that all the money we have or can get in France will be wanted for other more important purpose, therefore, I charge you not to expend one livre more than is absolutely necessary."

The "Alliance" sailed from Boston on December 23, 1781, and arrived at L'Orient, on January 18, 1782. During the voyage a British ship appeared in sight, "as if she could give them sport," as Barry's crew often wishing "Lafayette was in France," stated it. Barry's peremptory order to avoid all vessels and take no prizes debarred an encounter with the enemy. The crew manifested discontent at avoiding the possible prizes and, relates Kessler, this appeared to increase the conflict in Barry's mind between the call of duty and his inclination. Instead of reprobating and promptly punishing what on other occasions would have been the case, he was governed by a sullen silence which, if propriety permitted him to break, would have pronounced: "I also wish the Marquis were in France." But duty triumphed then as ever with Barry. As speedily as wind and wave and skill could force onward the "Alliance" she sped on her mission of the "utmost importance," and in twenty-three days Lafayette was in France.

Barry's instructions permitted him, after his placing Lafayette "in France," to cruise in search of prizes until March 1st. The "Alliance" sailed from L'Orient on February 10, 1782, and returned after seventeen days without making any captures, the vessels met being neutral ships.

On March 16, 1782, the "Alliance" sailed from L'Orient for return to America and here again disappointment came. All the vessels spoken on the voyage "none were of the enemy." On May 10th the "Alliance" arrived off the Delaware Bay. The British frigate "Chatham," of 64 guns, and the "Speedwell," sloop-of-war, barred entrance to the river, and off New York two more frigates joined in the chase of the "Alliance," but she, having a speed of fifteen knots an hour, succeeded in escaping the much superior force and getting to New London, Connecticut, on May 13th. This incident was one of traditionary interest among the veterans of the old time wooden navy.

"Not a prize this trip! Hard luck indeed," wrote Barry to John Brown, Secretary of the Board of Admiralty, to whom also he wrote that Robert Morris had sent him orders to join the French frigates at Rhode Island and be under their command. "Mr. Morris," wrote Barry, "must be unacquainted with his rank or he must think me a droll kind of a fellow to be commanded by a midshipman. I assure you I don't feel myself so low a commander as to brook such orders.

I suppose he will be much offended. I assure you although I serve the country for nothing I am determined no midshipman shall command me, let him be a chevalier or what he will."

Barry wrote from New London to Mr. Brown: "I never was in such a damn country in my life. You never was in so miserable a place in your life. All the people here live five miles from home. Not a house have I been in but the tavern and one Irishman's." The tavern was kept by Thomas Allen, an Irishman from the island of Antigua, whose "antipathy to the British was abnormal"—and so we may well believe he was a kindred spirit to that of Commodore Barry.

Though Captain Barry thought he had "hard luck" in not taking a prize, yet the log-book of the "Alliance," a copy of which he sent the Committee of Investigation, relates that on April 3d he fell in with two privateers, gave each of them a broadside, one of them struck, the other ran; hove out a signal for the "Marquis La Fayette" to take charge of the privateer that had struck while the "Alliance" went in chase of the other, "which we shortly after took." The record again shows Captain Barry did as he usually had done—captured two vessels in a battle.

Though he brought in no prize he yet was not unmindful of Mrs. Barry, but brought her a carpet and "a wash kettle full of claret," and doubtless other luxuries of the time as well as advising her "not to stay so much at home," as it "was clever to visit one's friends now and then, besides it is helpful to good health," added the gallant Captain.

CHAPTER XII.

A Most Successful Cruise—Nine Prizes.

The "Alliance" while at New London was fitted out for a cruise on which she started August 4, 1782, at four o'clock in the morning. Barry had a few days before an interview with General Washington. By seven o'clock Barry had captured from the enemy a brig laden with lumber and fish which "had been cut out of Rhode Island by the enemy." The cruise was first to the Bermudas and then to the Banks of New Foundland.

On August 9th Barry took the schooner "Polly" bound from Bermuda to Halifax with a cargo of molasses, sugar and lime and sent her to Boston. On August 19th arrived at the Bermudas after chasing several vessels, among which was the "Experiment," of 18 guns, which escaped into St. George's Harbor. On the 23d Barry sent Captain Tufts, of the "Polly," to inform the Governor that unless all the American prisoners were released he would remain for three weeks and hinder vessels going in or coming out which, said Barry, he "could effectively do as their whole force was not sufficient to cope with the 'Alliance.'" On August 25th Barry chased the privateer "Hawk" and took from her the sloop "Fortune," which she had captured. The "Hawk" escaped.

The "Alliance" continued cruising and chasing vessels until August 30th, when learning from a brig from Guadeloupe bound for Rhode Island, that a large fleet had sailed from Jamaica, Captain Barry concluded to attempt to overhaul by running northeast. On September 8th he captured a Nantucket brig returning from a whaling cruise. It had protection papers from Admiral Digby and permission to bring the oil to New York, then in British possession as during almost all the war. At this time the "Alliance" was off the Banks of New Foundland, where on September 18th the capture of a brig, one of the Jamaica fleet, was made. Barry learned that the convoy—the "Ramilie," of 74 guns—had foundered in a gale and that the fleet he was in search of had scattered.

The Story of Commodore John Barry

On September 24th Barry took two ships—on 27th he captured another. On the following day he captured a dismantled ship and all of the fleet from Jamaica he had been in search of and ordered them to L'Orient, France, where the "Alliance" with the prizes arrived October 17th, and the prisoners, except those who had entered into American service, were sent on shore. Most of the prisoners belonged at Glasgow where they had families. Otherwise these also would have entered under Captain Barry. "The separation," records Kessler, "was more like the separation of old friends than that of individuals of nations at war." Their treatment on the "Alliance" while prisoners was good. The officers were given quarters with officers—the privates placed with the privates of the "Alliance," enjoying fare alike. No confinement, no abridgment of food nor any labor required of them.

Several officers of the "Ramilie" were captives. The treatment they received from Captain Barry was so different from the usual treatment of American officers by the British commanders, it "made them blush for their country," notes Kessler, the Master's Mate. The captures numbered three ships, one snow, two brigs, one schooner and one sloop, all merchant vessels, variously loaded—nine prizes. Four other prizes were brought by the "Alliance" to L'Orient and four sent to America. They were sold at auction.

The shares of the United States as shown by Robert Morris' accounts were:

The "Kingston," 75,834.11.3 livres or $14,083.39

The "Commerce," 104,263.12.5 livres or $19,308.08.

The "Britannia," 43,620.18.5 livres or $8,077.85.

The "Anna," 71,656.11.5 livres or $13,269.60.

The prizes were loaded with rum, sugar, coffee and liquors. One-half the proceeds went to the Government—the other part to the captors. A Captain was entitled to six shares. Captain Barry's report of the cruise, dated October 18, 1782, reads: "A few hours after I sailed from New London I retook a brigantine and sent her in there; proceeded as fast as possible off Bermudas; on my way I took a schooner from that place for Halifax; after cruising off there for twelve or fifteen days I retook a sloop from New London and sent her to Cape François. Finding the prizes I had taken of little value either to myself or the country and in all likelihood should be obliged to return into port soon for want of men, was determined to alter my cruising ground. I, therefore, thought it best to run off the Banks of New Foundland. On my way thither I fell in with a whaling brigantine with a pass from Admiral Digby; I manned her and sent her to Boston. A few days after, off the Banks of New Foundland, I took a brigantine from Jamaica bound to London loaded with sugar and rum and sent her for Boston; by this vessel I found the Jamaica fleet was to the eastward of us. I then carried a press of sail for four days. The fifth day I took two ships that had parted with the fleet. After manning them, and a fresh gale westwardly, I thought best to order them to France. A day or two after I took a snow and a ship belonging to the same fleet.

"Being short of water, and a number of prisoners on board, the westwardly winds still blowing fresh and the expectation of falling in with some more of them, I thought it best to proceed to France, with a determined view to get those I had already taken in safe and after landing the prisoners to put out immediately; but meeting with blowing weather and high sea, I lost the sails of the head and was in great danger of losing the head, which accident obliged me to put in here, where I arrived yesterday with the four prizes. After repairing the damages and getting what the ships may want I shall put to sea on a cruise."

While at L'Orient, Captain Barry was invited by Lafayette to come to Paris, but as he had been "indisposed with a fever which confined him for ten days" and the ship ready to sail, he could not accept, but wrote the Marquis he envied the Captain who was to take him to America, but as that pleasure could not be his, Barry hoped to command the ship that would convey Lafayette back to France, when he would visit Paris and "have the honor of seeing Lady Fayette," an honor his brother who since was lost at sea had had.

CHAPTER XIII.

Officers of the "Alliance" Refuse to Serve—Peace.

Though in October Captain Barry hoped in a few days to proceed on a cruise it was not until December 8, 1782, that he was ready to sail, which he did the next day. Lieutenants Patrick Fletcher and Nicholas Gardner, John Buckley, Master; James Geagan, Surgeon, and Samuel Cooper, Purser, demanded two-thirds of their wages, "though they had received as much prize-money as they knew what to do with." Captain Barry informed them that he had no authority to pay them and had no money if he had. They refused to go on board the "Alliance" and do their duty. Accordingly, Captain Barry placed them under arrest until tried by Court-Martial in the United States. He was obliged to appoint others, "not adequate to the duty of the stations, 'but necessity knows no law,'" he wrote Thomas Barclay, Consul-General of the United States and Commissioner of the Navy in France, who justified Barry's course and concurred in the appointments he made.

All this time there were rumors of peace. On November 30, 1782, preliminary articles of peace had been signed. On December 5th King George III announced that he had given the "necessary orders to prohibit the further prosecution of offensive war upon the Continent of North America."

Though Captain Barry, early in December, 1782, had "great reason to think peace was concluded," he decided to make another cruise by "running down the coast of Guinea" and returning to America by way of Martinico, believing "should peace be made there will be a certain time given for vessels to make prizes in certain latitudes."

The "Alliance" sailed from L'Orient on December 9th, but though chasing several vessels, no encounter came about. On December 16th arrived at Porto Sancto—the next day the island of Madeira. Sailed hence and on January 8, 1783, arrived off Martinico. At St. Pierre

The Story of Commodore John Barry

Harbor Barry found orders for him to proceed to Havana to take in specie for Congress.

On January 12th sailed for Havana and after stopping at St. Eustatia and Cape François arrived there January 17th. While off Hispaniola Barry met an English fleet of seventeen sail, but he "got clear of them." The next day met two British cruisers, one of 74 guns. They chased the "Alliance" under the guns of Cape François.

On February 13th Captain Barry notified the Governor of Havana that the "Alliance" and "Duc de Lauzun," frigates belonging to Congress, were ready to sail from that port. He requested permission for the frigates to depart as he had "despatches from the Court of France which are very important," and also desired that the American merchant vessels at the port should be permitted to depart under convoy of the "Alliance." The Governor replied that, complying with secret instructions from the King, it was entirely out of his power to grant the permission sought. To which Barry replied that it was somewhat singular for ships of war employed on national objects to be restricted in the same manner as merchant vessels. He then again asked "in the name of my Sovereign for permission for the sailing of the two American ships of war." He withdrew his request for the trading vessels as they were "fully under the influence of the embargo." The Governor replied that he and the Admiral of the Squadron had consulted and decided that permission could not be given then. He advised Captain Barry "to reflect on the immense prejudice that might occur to the common cause of the allied powers and commerce of Spain if any unlucky accident should happen by the enemy taking one of the frigates."

On February 22d, Washington's birthday, Captain Barry issued orders "to exercise the great guns and the small arms every day, to loose the topsails in order the men could learn to do it well, to have wood and water ready for sea." He evidently was having the ship ready for service and action though he had brought the news of peace to the West India Islands.

CHAPTER XIV.

The Last Battle of the Revolution.

Captain Barry's foresight in having everything ready for war, although the preliminary articles of peace had been signed, was soon manifested. The "Alliance" left Havana on March 6, 1783, in company with the "Duc de Lauzun," commanded by Captain Greene. There also sailed nine Spanish warships. Not knowing where the Spaniards were bound to, Captain Barry decided to make his own way and ordered Captain Greene to follow him.

The "Alliance" and "Lauzun" had seventy-two thousand dollars "of public money on board," which Captain Barry had been entrusted with to deliver, by order of Robert Morris, Superintendent of Finance, to George Olney, of Providence, R.I., in case he arrived in that harbor. The afternoon after leaving Havana two British cruisers were seen. Captains Barry and Greene "stood for the Spanish fleet," of which some vessels had been seen in the morning. He did this as "the only way to save the 'Lauzun,'" as that vessel sailed "much heavier" than the "Alliance." At ten o'clock at night they got in sight of part of the Spanish fleet. The British men-of-war had followed closely and had got within gun-shot of the "Alliance" and "Lauzun" when, observing the lights of the Spaniards, they abandoned the chase. Barry and Greene kept in company with the Spaniards all night—though they found in the morning that they were but eight or ten sloops and schooners. "However, they answered our ends," reported Captain Barry.

The British not being in sight and no tidings of them among the Spaniards, the Americans "made the best of their way." Finding the "Lauzun" much slower than the "Alliance," the public money on board of her was transferred to the "Alliance." On the morning of the 9th "three large sail of ships," British men-of-war, were seen "standing directly for us," reported Barry. He signaled Greene to follow him, who replied the enemy were of superior force. The "Alliance" having the money, Barry believing he could be of no service to the "Lauzun," made all sail and ran faster than the British could follow. But Barry shortened sail and spoke the "Lauzun." By this time one of the British, a 32-gun frigate, was within gun-shot of the "Alliance" and the "Lauzun"—the other two British cruisers a little way astern and fast coming up to the "Lauzun." Captain Greene told Captain Barry the two were privateers, but Barry "told him he was mistaken" and that he knew better.

While the "Alliance" dropped astern, the foremost British frigate shortened sail and would not come near the "Alliance."

Later the two British came up fast. Captain Barry, "confident within" himself that the "Alliance" "would have fallen a sacrifice" if he remained with the "Lauzun," signaled Captain Greene to heave his guns overboard so as to get clear of the enemy by lightening his ship. By this time one of the British was within gun-shot of the "Lauzun." They fired several shots at one another but at too great a distance for either to do damage. In the morning a strange ship had been seen to the southward, but sailing away from the "Alliance." In the afternoon after the "Lauzun" had exchanged shots with the enemy pursuing her, this "strange sail" stood for the Americans. Barry had "all the reason in the world to suppose she was a stranger to the enemy also," as at that time the "Lauzun" was firing "stern chasers" at her pursuer. Barry then ran down between the "Lauzun" and the enemy in order to give Captain Greene a chance to get off by bringing the enemy into action, which Barry did "close on board for forty-five minutes, when the enemy sheered off." During the action the "Alliance" had ten wounded—one dying later. The "spars and rigging were hurt a little but not so much but they would all do again." Captains Barry and Greene then sailed towards the strange ship. It proved to be a French gun ship of 60 guns, which had sailed from Havana two days before Barry and Greene. It had half a million dollars on board and was bound to one of the French islands.

Kessler relates that Captain Barry expected the French gunship to assist the "Alliance"; that two of the British kept "at a distance as if waiting to ascertain about the French ship." But though she "approached the Americans fast," she did not join in the encounter.

The Story of Commodore John Barry

When Captain Barry afterwards "asked them why they did not come down during the action, they answered they thought they might have been taken, and the signal known; that the action was only 'a sham to decoy him.'"

"His foolish action," records Kessler, "thus, perhaps, lost us the three frigates, for Captain Barry commenced the action in the full expectation of the French ship joining and thereby not only be able to cope but to subdue part, if not the whole of them."

The French proposed to give chase. This was done, but the French ship could not keep up with the "Alliance" or the slower "Lauzun." This battle took place on March 10, 1783. The British frigate was the "Sybille," commanded by Captain Vashon, which, on January 22, 1783, had been captured from the French by the British "Hussar," commanded by Captain Thomas Macnamara Russell. Captain Vashon "confessed he had never seen a ship so ably fought as the 'Alliance,' that he had never received such a drubbing and was indebted to his consorts for his escape from capture." He always spoke of Captain Barry in the most magnanimous terms.

"The coolness and intrepidity no less than the skill and fertility in expedients which Captain Barry displayed on this occasion are described in naval annals as truly wonderful; every quality of a great commander was brought out with extraordinary brilliancy."

This is the occasion on which Captain Barry is said to have replied to the hail of the British that his was "The United States ship 'Alliance,' Saucy Jack Barry, half Irishman, half Yankee! Who are you?"

I do not believe this true. It is too bombastic to suit the character of Captain Barry. He could not have called himself "Saucy," for nothing of impetuosity or dare-devilishness was ever manifested in his career. Nor did he ever flippantly call himself "Jack."

"My name is John Barry," was his dignified declaration to Lieutenant Gregory, as we have seen. It embodied respect and determination and dignity of character which he ever maintained.

Let not his admirers lessen that dignity.

This—the last battle of the Revolution—occurred March 10, 1783, after the signing of the Provisional Articles of Peace at Paris, November 30, 1782; after the Preliminary Articles for Restoring Peace, signed at Versailles on January 20, 1783, and also after the Ratification of the Preliminary Articles on February 3, 1783, by the Ministers of the United States, France and Great Britain, by which a cessation of hostilities was agreed upon.

On April 11, 1783, Congress, by Proclamation, ordered the "cessation of arms as well by sea as by land." But, one month prior, Captain John Barry had the final encounter on the ocean in defense of the Liberty and Independence of the United States. He had thus commanded the first Continental cruiser, the "Lexington" and also commanded the last Continental frigate, the "Alliance"; bringing to Congress the first prize brought to Philadelphia and defending and saving the last Continental war money brought to the country on the last armed vessel of the new Nation. He commanded the "Lexington," the first vessel commissioned by authority of the Continental Congress. He commanded the "Alliance," the best vessel the Congress had commissioned and the last in the Continental service. He brought Congress its first prize. He brought Congress its last war money.

On March 20, 1783, the "Alliance" arrived at Newport, R.I.—the last war day, as on the next day the "Triumphe," commanded by Chevalier du Quesne, arrived at Philadelphia with the preliminary Treaty of Peace. She had been despatched from Cadiz on February 11th by D'Estaing, who was ready to sail with sixty ships of the line and a very formidable armament, but had given up the voyage on the agreement for peace.

On March 25th—Annunciation Day—Congress ordered the recall of all vessels cruising under authority of the United States.

On April 19, 1783, Washington announced the close of the war and the disbandment of the army.

On April 16th the cessation of hostilities was proclaimed in Barry's home city—Philadelphia—to "a vast concourse of people, who expressed their satisfaction on the happy occasion by repeated shouts. The State flag was hoisted and the bells were rung and a general joy diffused itself throughout the city."

New York City had been under British control nearly the whole war. How great the contrast there. "When the proclamation was read nothing but groans and hisses prevailed, attended by bitter reproaches and curses on their King for having deserted them in the midst of their calamities."

Philadelphia, the seat of the "Rebellion," now by success made a "Revolution," was open to the commerce of the world. On May 2d the ship "Hibernia," Robert Scallan, Master, arrived from Dublin and soon, at the store of Clement Biddle his cargo of "gold and silver silks, rich and slight brocades, flannels, Mantuas and fabrics, colored and sky colored tissue and Florentines, tamboured silks and satin, shapes for gentlemen's vests and black Norwich capes" were on sale.

Joy bounded throughout the land. Meetings were held to express patriotic sentiments. The men of Northampton, Pa., did so. The ladies of Northampton followed the next day. Among the "toasts" on the occasion was this: "May the Protestant religion prevail and flourish through all nations."

Yet John Barry, an Irish-born Roman Catholic, had battled all the eight years—from the first to the last of the fight—to win Freedom and Independence for the land in which these Ladies of Northampton "hoped the Protestant religion might prevail."

The Story of Commodore John Barry

THE FRIGATE "UNITED STATES"

CHAPTER XV.

BARRY VISITS THE "SYBILLE" ON HIS RETURN TO PHILADELPHIA— PEACE IS DECLARED—ORDERED TO AMSTERDAM WITH TOBACCO—THE "ALLIANCE" BECOMES DISABLED—IS ORDERED SOLD.

After Captain Barry had arrived at New London it was nearly three months before he came on to Philadelphia. Mrs. Barry had, in April, gone on to New London. Captain Barry returned home by way of New York. The "Sybille" was there. Captain Barry visited her and was "politely treated" by Captain Vashon. The vessel yet bore the marks of the injury Barry had inflicted and "they said they had not been treated so roughly before," records Kessler. Some of the Hessians were embarked on her for return home. As she had received "eighteen cannon shots her condition was such that pumps had to be manned night and day to keep her from filling five to eight feet of water." That proved how she had been shattered by Barry. Captain Barry, after a brief visit to Philadelphia, returned to Providence Harbor and soon set sail for the Rappahannock River, Virginia, for a cargo of tobacco for Amsterdam, Holland, on public account, to pay the interest on loan negotiated there. This was in August, 1783.

On the way down the Providence River the "Alliance," when going four or five miles an hour, ran against a sunken rock, which "stopped her as quick as thought," related Barry. After remaining on the rock two hours and finding the ship made no water in consequence of the mishap, the "Alliance" proceeded to Virginia where she took on 500 hogsheads of tobacco weighing 530,000 pounds.

The Accounts of Robert Morris show that to meet this Holland Loan, 1837 hogsheads of tobacco weighing 1,937,355 pounds had been sent by Daniel Clarke, Agent of the Finance Department.

The Story of Commodore John Barry

On August 24th the "Alliance" sailed from the Capes of Virginia "with good prospects before us and in hopes of a short voyage. But," as Captain Barry reported to Robert Morris on the 26th from the Delaware Bay, "as is often the case when people's expectations are buoyed up with great prospects they frequently find themselves disappointed."

"We had not been long out with a moderate breeze, wind and smooth sea when we discovered all of a sudden the ship to make nineteen inches per hour and soon to have three feet of water in her hold and so damaging the tobacco."

Captain Barry then "made for the Delaware." Though her bottom was "perfectly sound when bore down at Providence," Barry believed the run on the rock caused the leak. The damage to the "Alliance" was serious enough to warrant Congress appointing a committee to examine the condition of the ship. On September on their report Congress ordered the ship "to be unladen and her cargo freighted to Europe on the best terms." The Agent of Marine was directed to discharge officers and crew, have her surveyed and a report made of the expense "necessary to give her a good repair." Five hundred hogsheads of the tobacco were reshipped on the "Princess Ulrico" [480 hhds.] and the "Four Friends" [20 hhds.].

Had the voyage to Amsterdam been made, Barry would have stopped at London. Robert Morris gave him a (July 24, 1783) letter of introduction to Messrs. Bewickes & Mourgue of that city stating that: "He has proved himself a brave and deserving officer in the service of his country and a worthy man in every station of life." (Crimmin's Autographs.) He also had a letter from John Paul Jones to friends in Paris.

In pursuance of the Act, Robert Morris, Agent of Marine, appointed as surveyors Captains John Barry and Thomas Read and Messrs. Thomas Penrose, Joshua Humphreys, Jr., and Benjamin G. Eyre. The latter were shipbuilders. They estimated the repairs would cost 5866-2/3 dollars—that it was not necessary to keep the "Alliance" for the protection of commerce and it would be to the interest of the Union to dispose of her. A resolution to direct the Agent of Marine to dispose of her by public auction was adopted on June 3, 1785. She was sold on August 1, 1785. So Congress parted with its last and its best vessel. The new Nation was without a ship or flag on the ocean. Captain Barry had the first Continental vessel. He commanded the last one. Great must have been his satisfaction when given the "Lexington." Sad, indeed, must he have been in parting with the "Alliance."

She was purchased by Coburn & Whitehead for £2287 or $7,700 in certificates of public credit. They sold to Robert Morris "at a great profit." She became a merchant vessel and in June, 1787, made a voyage to China, returning September, 1788. She was of 724 tons—a large ship for those days. After all her perilous voyages and wonderful escapes from the enemy she was beached on Petty's Island in the Delaware River opposite Kensington, Philadelphia. Part of her timbers remained until 1901 and her hulk was visible at low tide. The widening of the channel caused the removal of what remained of her hulk. Pieces are preserved at the Museum of Independence Hall, where it is labeled as having been commanded by John Paul Jones. Another portion is at the American Catholic Historical Society of Philadelphia. There also may be seen the card table and soup tureen of the Commodore, deposited by the compiler of this record.

CHAPTER XVI.

AFTER THE WAR BARRY SECURES THE ADOPTION OF THE NEW FEDERAL CONSTITUTION BY FORCING A QUORUM OF THE ASSEMBLY—IS SUED—GOES TO CHINA IN COMMAND OF THE "ASIA," A MERCHANT VESSEL.

After the sale of the "Alliance," Captain Barry "rested from his labors," but yet concerned about many things pertaining to his friends and their interests. We find him recommending subordinate officers for positions in the merchant service, in petitioning Congress that officers of the Navy be put on "a footing similar to their brother officers of the land service, as to half-pay or commutation and lands according to their ranks, as they were the only class of officers who remain neglected and totally unprovided for." He referred evidently to his own experience when he said, "few of the ships belonging to the United States were ever suffered to cruise, but were sent on private service and ordered not to go out of their way, but to keep clear of all vessels whatever and that such as were permitted had particular cruising grounds pointed out to them, which frequently ensured them severe blows and but few prizes."

When in 1787 a Federal convention had been held in Philadelphia to formulate a Constitution by which the States could form "a more perfect union" and "promote domestic tranquility," the present Constitution of our country was formulated by the convention for ratification by the several States. In each State controversy and discussion arose over the consideration of the advisability of adopting it as the supreme law of the land.

The Confederation had proven unsuited to the needs of the country. So a new plan of government was necessary. On September 17th, the day the Convention had adopted the Constitution, the Pennsylvania members of the Convention at once notified the Assembly of the State, then in session at the Hall of Independence, that they were ready to report to the Assembly. The next morning "the honorable delegates, led by Benjamin Franklin, were ushered into the Hall of

The Story of Commodore John Barry

the Assembly, made their report and presented the new Constitution." No action was taken by the Assembly. On September 29th, the last day but one of the session, George Clymer proposed to refer the Act of Ratification to a Convention of the State. Pleas for delay were made. Thomas FitzSimons, a Catholic, one of the Representatives at the Constitutional Convention and also a member of the Pennsylvania Assembly, opposed delay in submitting the new Constitution to a convention of the citizens for adoption or rejection.

It was resolved to call a State Convention, but no day was fixed for its meeting. Nineteen members had voted against calling it. On their behalf it was asked that the consideration of the time of the meeting of the convention should be postponed until the afternoon. This was granted. When the House again met, the nineteen were absent. The Assembly lacked a quorum. The absentees were sent for, but refused to appear. Mr. Wynkoop declared: "If there is no way of compelling those who deserted from duty to perform it, then God be merciful to us!"

There was a way of "compelling" and Captain John Barry led the compellers.

The next morning a number of citizens, whose leader was Commodore John Barry, forcibly entered the lodgings of James McCalmont and Jacob Miley, the members from Franklin and Dauphin Counties, dragged them to the State House and thrust them into the chamber where the Assembly was in session without a quorum. With these two there were forty-six representatives present—a quorum. Mr. McCalmont informed the House that he had been forcibly brought into the Assembly-room, contrary to his wishes, by a number of citizens. He begged he might be allowed to retire.

Thomas FitzSimons replied that if any member of the House had forced the gentleman from the determination to absent himself, such member's conduct met the disapprobation of the House. But Mr. McCalmont was now here and the business of the State cannot be accomplished if any one is suffered to withdraw.

The Story of Commodore John Barry

When Mr. McCalmont attempted to leave he was restrained by the citizens who had "dragged" him into the Assembly. The House resumed the fixing a time for the Convention to act on the Constitution. The date was fixed. The people cheered. Christ Church chimes rang and Captain Barry, we may be sure, was happy. By his action within twenty-three hours of the adoption of the Constitution by the Federal Convention, Pennsylvania had ordered a State Convention to consider it. Verses relative to the "dragging" were soon published. One extract recited:

"It seems to me I yet see Barry
Drag out McCalmont."

But McCalmont undertook the "dragging" of Barry into Court. On October 13, 1787, he applied to the Supreme Executive Council and the Council directed the Attorney-General to commence a prosecution against "Captain John Barry and such other persons as shall be found to have been principally active in seizing James McCalmont or otherwise concerned in the riotous proceedings." Ben Franklin, President, was one of the eight who voted for the resolution. The Attorney-General began suit but at the Council meeting, February 16, 1788, he requested the advice of the Council "relative to the suit carried on by their order against Captain John Barry." The Council informed him it did not wish to interfere, but left the matter with him to do as he judged best.

So nothing more was done about the suit. By this time Captain Barry was on the high seas on his way to China in the merchant ship "Asia," in which he had sailed on January 7, 1787. It returned to Philadelphia, June 4, 1789. So Captain Barry had been away over two years. Eight years afterwards, on July 7, 1797, the "Asia," commanded by Captain Yard, when returning from Bengal, was captured in sight of Cape May, New Jersey, by the Spanish privateer "Julia," commanded by Don Baptista Mahon, a name indicating Irish descent. She was valued at $800,000. But the next month she was recaptured by an American privateer off Havana.

The Story of Commodore John Barry

Columbia claims her soldier love and Ireland joys to own
The boy who sailed from his Wexford home undaunted if unknown;
Columbia guards his latest sleep—hers was his manhood's noon.
Ireland's the vigorous cradling arms and tender cradle croon;
For Ireland paints the dreaming boy on the lonely Wexford shore,
In 'customed clasp may meet the hands of mother and foster-mother
Above his grave, who was loyal to each as each unto the other.

—*Margaret M. Halvey.*

CHAPTER XVII.

CAPTAIN BARRY OFFERS HIS SERVICES TO PRESIDENT WASHINGTON IN CASE OF WAR AGAINST THE ALGERINES.

In 1793 France and England engaged in war, seized each other's vessels on the American coast and often within American waters. The Algerines were committing depredations on American commerce. Hence a naval force was necessary. When Congress assembled in December, 1793, the building of frigates early engaged attention, not only to protect commerce from the ravages of the Algerines but from the aggressions of France as well as from the violation of our neutrality by England.

The United States was without a ship.

Captain John Barry was prompt to offer his services to his country.

On March 19, 1794, he wrote President Washington:

"*Sir*:—Finding that the Government have partly determined to fit out some ships of war for the protection of our trade against the Algerines, I beg leave to offer myself for the command of the squadron, conceiving myself to be competent, thereto assuring your Excellency that should I be honored with your approbation, my utmost abilities and most unremitting attention should be exerted for the good of my country and also to approve myself worthy of the high honor shown by your Excellency.

"To your Obedient, Humble Servant,
"March 19, 1794.

John Barry

"HIS EXCELLENCY.

A week later, March 27, 1794, Washington signed an Act declaring that "the depredations of the Algerine Corsairs on the commerce of the United States rendered it necessary that a naval force should be provided for its protection."

This Act is the foundation of our present Navy.

Congress ordered the building and equipment of three frigates of forty-four guns and three of lesser weight and tonnage.

On June 5, 1794, public announcement was made of the appointment of six Captains to superintend the construction and to take command of the vessels thus ordered. The notice sent to Captain Barry read:

"WAR DEPARTMENT, June 5, 1794.

"*Sir*:—The President of the United States, by and with the advice and consent of the Senate, has appointed you to be a Captain of one of the ships provided, in pursuance of the Act to provide a naval armament, herein enclosed.

"It is understood that the relative rank of the Captains is to be in the following order:

John Barry,
Samuel Nicholson,
Silas Talbot,
Joshua Barney,
Richard Dale,
Thomas Truxtun.

You will please to inform me as soon as convenient whether you accept or decline the appointment.

"I am, Sir, etc.,

"To "HENRY KNOX,
CAPTAIN BARRY." *Secretary of War*.

Captain Barry at once accepted, saying:

"STRAWBERRY HILL, June 6, 1794.

"The honor done me in appointing me Commander in the Navy of the United States is gratefully acknowledged and accepted by,

Sir,
Your Most Obedient,
Humble Servant,

John Barry

The original is in the Force Collection in the Lenox Branch of the New York Public Library.

The commission was not signed nor issued by Washington until February 22, 1797, when the frigate the "United States," built under the superintendency of Barry, was ready for launching at Philadelphia. The original commission is in possession of Barry's grand-niece, Mrs. W. Horace Hepburn, of Philadelphia.

Captain Barney declined appointment because of the rank—the fourth—assigned him. Captain James Sever was appointed but given the sixth place. Captain Nicholson, at Boston, on June 14, 1794, congratulated Captain Barry on his "honorable appointment to the Command of our Navy."

"Captain Barry," says Cooper's *History of the Navy*, "was the only one of the six surviving Captains of the Revolutionary War who was not born in America, but he had passed nearly all his life in it and was thoroughly identified with his adopted countrymen in interest and feeling. He had often distinguished himself during the Revolution and, perhaps, of all the naval Captains that remained, he was the one who possessed the greatest reputation for experience, conduct and skill. His appointment met with general approbation. Nor did anything ever occur to give the Government reason to regret its selection."

The Story of Commodore John Barry

So the County Wexford Irish Catholic boy had become the Commander-in-Chief of the new Navy of the new Constitutional United States. Appointed by Washington, "the Father of His Country," Barry thus became "the Father of the American Navy," in the many distinguished sons of the sea who were trained under him.

His commission reads, "to take rank from the fourth day of June, one thousand seven hundred and ninety-four."

There are gallant hearts whose glory
Columbia loves to name,
Whose deeds shall live in story
And everlasting fame.
But never yet one braver
Our starry banner bore
Than saucy old Jack Barry
The Irish Commodore.

—*William Collins.*

CHAPTER XVIII.

APPOINTED TO SUPERINTEND THE BUILDING OF THE FRIGATE, THE "UNITED STATES," THE FIRST OF THE NEW NAVY—GOES TO GEORGIA TO SELECT TIMBER FOR THE FOUR FRIGATES.

On April 12, 1794, Joshua Humphreys, of Philadelphia, was directed by General Knox, Secretary of War—there was no Department of the Navy until 1798—to prepare models for the frame of the frigates to be built. On June 28th, Humphreys was appointed "Constructor or Master-Builder of a 44-gun ship to be built at the port of Philadelphia at the rate of $2000 per annum—the compensation commencing on the 1st of May last, in consideration of your incessant application to the public interest in adjusting the principles of the ships, drawing drafts and making moulds, etc."

On August 7th, General Knox notified Captain Barry: "You are to consider yourself as the Superintendent of the frigate to be built at the port of Philadelphia and which is to mount 44 guns." This frigate was named the "United States." It was built on the Delaware River at the foot of [now] Washington Avenue near the old Swedes Church. It was constructed mainly of Georgia live oak, "the most durable wood in the world," selected by Captain Barry who, in October, 1794, by direction of Tench Coxe, Commissioner of the Revenues, proceeded to that State for that purpose, sailing on the brig "Schuylkill" which carried oxen and horses which were "of the highest importance to the expediting of the timber for the several frigates," to which Captain Barry was to give all possible exertions "to the cutting and transportation of the timber for his own and every other frigate."

On October 14th the "Schuylkill" arrived at Gashayes Bluff, on the island of St. Simon, where he found Mr. John T. Morgan, superintendent of cutting the timber, but not "a stick of wood cut." Barry sent him "into the country to try and get hands." He got six. Barry succeeded in getting ten more. So that on the 20th Morgan set the sixteen at work. On the 22d eighty-one woodcutters arrived from

The Story of Commodore John Barry

New London. They were set to work. Barry after "doing all in his power at St. Simon's" went to Savannah to charter a vessel—returned to St. Simon's and thence to Philadelphia, wherefrom, he, on November 10th, reported to Commissioner Coxe.

On December 12th he presented his bill of expenses for "Voyage to Georgia on Public Account." He had been given $200. His expenses amounted to $124.24. So he returned $75.76.

His salary as Captain of the Navy was $75 a month.

Captains Barry, Dale and Truxtun on December 18, 1794, wrote the Secretary of War that the frigates could be built and equipped next year, adding, "It would be highly gratifying to us who have thrown aside our former occupations and the prospects that were fair for increasing our fortunes, with a view of serving our country, and who have no desire of being mere sinecure officers if we could at this moment embark and obey the commands of our country, in going in pursuit of a barbarous enemy, who now holds in chains and slavery so many of our unfortunate fellow-citizens; the relieving and restoring of which to the bosom of their families and friends are, with that of having an opportunity to chastise their cruel oppressors, objects of our greatest ambition and which we anticipate with all the ardor of officers, of seamen and of citizens."

But no haste was made in building the frigates. Temporary diplomatic arrangements with France quieted or averted action. Our country paid tribute to the Barbary State and sent barrels of silver to purchase tolerance on the sea from these pirates as a cheaper method of peace than the cost and maintenance of armed vessels of war would be.

By the Act of March 27, 1794, work on the frigates was to cease in the event of peace being signed with Algiers. So when on December 21, 1795, Washington informed the Senate that the Emperor of Morocco had signed a treaty of peace and friendship with the United States, work on the frigates was suspended. Washington called the attention of Congress to the loss that would come if the work ceased, whereupon on April 20, 1796, Congress ordered the unexpended balance to be used, but ordered the work to be discontinued. Yet President Washington in his message had declared: "To secure respect for a neutral flag requires a naval force organized and ready to vindicate it from insult or aggression.... Our trade to the Mediterranean, without a protecting force, will always be insecure. Will it not then be advisable to begin without delay to provide and lay up materials for the building and equipping of ships of war and to proceed with the work by degrees, in proportion as our resources shall render it practicable, without inconvenience so that a future war of Europe may not find our commerce in the unprotected state in which it was found by the present."

The cannon for the frigates had been cast at Cecil Furnace, Maryland. Captain Barry, on May 16, 1796, was sent there "to see the guns and examine whether they were suitable or fit for service."

The frigate "United States" was progressing rapidly towards completion. Captain Barry, on September 19, 1796, estimated the cost of fitting out for officers and men at $7285. The vessel when completed cost $299,336. She was 175 feet in length, 44 feet beam and of 1576 tonnage. She was launched May 10, 1797.

"In the long list of splendid vessels which in a hundred combats have maintained the honor of our national flag, the 'United States' stands at the head." She served our country well in the war with France under Barry; also in the war with England in 1812-15 and in subsequent duties, peaceful or warlike.

LINES ON THE DEATH OF COMMODORE BARRY.

BY MICHAEL FORTUNE.

Columbia's friend, freed from this worldly coil,
Now rests (so Heav'n ordains) from human toil;
A Patriot firm, thro' chequer'd life unblam'd,
A gallant vet'ran, for his powers fam'd.
Beneath his guidance, lo! a Navy springs,

The Story of Commodore John Barry

An infant Navy spreads its canvas wings,
A rising Nation's weal, to shield, to save,
And guard her Commerce on the dang'rous wave.

Whoe'er the Sage, his character shall scan,
Must trace those Virtues that exalt the man,
The bold achievement and heroic deed
To honor's fame, the laurel'd Brave that lead,
Long for his merits and unsully'd name
(Dear to his friends and sanctify'd name);
His clay cold relics shall his country mourn,
And with her tears bedew his hallow'd urn.

Come, cheering Hope—celestial cherub come—
Say that his virtues soar beyond the tomb,
Say that with Mercy in ethereal guise,
His white-robed spirit climbs yon op'ning skies.

(Philadelphia, Sept., 1803.)

CHAPTER XIX.

Launch of the "United States"—War with France—Barry Commands the American Fleet in the West Indies—Captures the "San Pareil"—Again sent to the West Indies—Barry Fires on the French Batteries at Basse Terre—To France Again—Death of Our Hero.

The frigate "United States" though launched in May, 1797, was not ready for sea until July, 1798, when, on 3d July, the new Secretary of the new Department—the Navy—Hon. Benjamin Stoddert, directed Captain Barry "to proceed to sea with the first fair wind," and expressing President Adams' "conviction that nothing on your part will be wanting to justify the high confidence reposed by him and your country in your activity, skill and bravery."

He was directed to cruise "from Cape Henry to Nantucket," to "defend this extent of coast against the depredations of the vessels sailing under authority or pretence of authority of the French Republic," and to "afford all possible protection to the vessels of the United States coming on or going off the coast," in conjunction with Captain Dale. Captain Barry was authorized "to subdue, seize and take any armed French vessel which should be found within the jurisdictional limits of the United States or elsewhere on the high seas, with apparel, guns and appurtenances." On July 11, 1798, Secretary Stoddert notified Barry that information was received that "the French have considerable force in the West Indies" and that "it is thought that a small squadron under the command of an officer of your intelligence, experience and bravery might render essential service and animate your country to enterprise by picking up a number of prizes in the short cruise of these islands."

So Barry was directed to take the "Delaware," Captain Stephen Decatur; the "Herald," Captain Sever, and a revenue cutter of 14 guns from Boston "and to proceed to the West Indies and so dispose of the vessels as to afford the greatest chance of falling in with French armed vessels," to "look into St. John's, the principal harbor of Porto Rico and after two or three days' cruising, return to the continent."

"The object of the enterprise," said the Secretary, "is to do as much injury to the armed vessels of France and to make as many captures as possible." He closed saying, "It is scarcely necessary for me, in writing to a brave man who values his own country, its government and its laws, to suggest the usefulness of inculcating upon those under his command the propriety of preserving in their language and conduct the same respect which he himself feels for those constitutions and those characters which deserve the respect of all. It is time we should establish an American character. Let that character be a love of country and a jealousy of its honor. This idea comprehends everything that ought to be impressed upon the minds of all our citizens, but more especially of those citizens who are seamen and soldiers."

Barry was directed, when at St. John [San Juan], to write the Governor requesting that the American seamen who had collected there to return to the United States should be permitted to do so, but as the United States was at peace with Spain no hostile measures were to be taken to obtain them if the civil authorities should not produce them. Barry and Decatur sailed northward and off the coast of New England. On July 26, 1798, they sailed for the West Indies, the revenue cutter not being ready to proceed with them. The "United States" and the "Delaware" returned to Philadelphia September 21, 1798. Captain Barry had captured the French schooner "Le Jaleux," of 14 guns and 70 men and also the "San Pareil," of 10 guns and 67 men, belonging to Guadeloupe. The "San Pareil," in 1794, captured the vessel on which Charles and Catharine, children of Charles Carroll, of Carrollton, were returning from England. Proceeding to the West Indies the "San Pareil" fell in with the "Pallas" bound to the Kennebeck and compelled her to take the passengers and crew to Boston. [Rowland's *Carroll* II, p. 200.]

Now Barry had captured the "San Pareil." The crews were imprisoned at New Castle, Del., until November 6th, where it was alleged, by opponents of the Adams administration, they were cruelly treated by being neglected and uncared for. "The government allowed nothing, though it furnished blankets. The French Consul had neither funds nor orders to give his countrymen relief." Secretary Stoddert, then resident at Trenton, New Jersey, because of the yellow fever, wrote President Adams, at Quincy, Massachusetts, that "Barry returned too soon. His reason, apprehensions from the hurricanes in the West Indies at this season. Upon the whole, it is better than to have kept the ships sleeping on our own shore, though the result of the enterprise falls very far short of my hopes."

Yet the Secretary had when reporting to the President that Barry had been sent to the West Indies "to be employed while the French have but little force" and that "the hurricane season" was near, had yet "hopes" that neither Barry nor Decatur had been able to satisfy. By direction of the President both were, on September 28, 1798, sent out again—"Decatur to cruise from the Delaware to Cape Henry and Barry to cruise from the Delaware along the eastern coast northward"—though the Secretary had informed the President "it is not to be apprehended that our coasts will be much molested by French cruisers," as they had no force in the West Indies equal to ours "and it was not probable they could send a force from Europe." Barry and Decatur were ordered to return about November 15th. Barry on the cruise was "to protect the trade from Delaware to New Hampshire, while Decatur did the same from New York to the Chesapeake."

Barry sailed from New Castle on October 8th without "a single article for the ship but ballast and," so he wrote Mrs. Barry, "my reason for going to sea without these is the European ships are expected any day and should any of them be taken and I lying in the harbor, the merchants may blame me and no other, although it would not be my fault." Barry returned on November 9th "totally unexpected," as an "accident had prevented the 'United States' from getting to Newport," where the ship had been expected to appear.

The Story of Commodore John Barry

On November 29, 1798, Captains Barry, Dale, Truxtun and Tingley were directed to report upon "a proper system for the government of the Navy." He had previously recommended the establishment of Navy Yards and organization of a Navy Department. The War Department had, previous to 1798, directed all naval affairs. At the opening of Congress in December, 1798, President Adams, in his Message, declared the law of France, that "neutral vessels with British fabrics or produce, although the entire property belonging to neutrals, were liable to seizure," was an "unequivocal act of war on the commerce of the nation it attacks," and so "whether we negotiate with her or not, a vigorous preparation for war will be alike indispensable." He urged the increase of the Navy. Congress in February, 1799, added six 74's and six 18's to the naval force at a cost of $2,400,000. The naval appropriation for 1799 amounted to $4,594,677.

On December 7, 1798, Captain Barry was placed in "immediate command" of the frigates the "United States," the "Constitution," the "George Washington," the "Merrimac" with four or five more vessels of nearly the same force as the latter (24 guns). The fleet was to be employed in the West Indies in active operations for the "protection of our commerce and for the capture or destruction of French armed vessels from St. Christopher's as far as Barbadoes and Tobago," and to "pay considerable attention to Cayenne and Curricoa and even to the passage from the United States to Laguayra, on the Spanish Main, to which place our citizens carry on considerable trade," but above all, Barry was "to relieve our commerce from the piccaroons and pirates continually issuing from the Island of Guadeloupe."

Captain Truxtun was assigned "from St. Christopher's to Porto Rico," with two or three vessels of 14 and 18 guns. Captain Decatur, with one brig of 16 guns, "the vicinity of Havana," and Captain Tingley in the "Ganges," "between Cuba and Hispaniola," to give security to the trade of Jamaica.

The Story of Commodore John Barry

The expedition was designed "to rid those seas as well of French armed vessels as of the pirates which infest them."

Barry was directed to "proceed as early as possible to Prince Rupert's Bay in the Island of Dominica, where the other vessels" of his command were ordered to rendezvous and he was to "commence operations." Under Barry's command on this expedition were Charles Stewart, Stephen Decatur, Jacob Jones, all of whom became famous in naval annals and obtained the highest positions. Barry's training and discipline developed heroes after his death. When the squadron reached the West Indies, Barry's command consisted of the frigate "United States," the "Constitution," Captain Samuel Nicholson; the "George Washington," Captain Patrick Fletcher; the "Merrimac," Captain Moses Brown; the "Portsmouth," Captain Daniel McNeill; the "Pickering," Master-Commandant Edward Preble; the "Eagle," Lieutenant Hugh George Campbell; the "Herald," Lieutenant Charles Russell; the "Scammel," Lieutenant J. Adams, and the "Diligence," Lieutenant J. Brown. The vessels sailing from Norfolk, Virginia, in company with Barry's frigate the "United States" were the "Constellation," of 36 guns; the "John Adams," the "Congress," the "Little Adams," the "Little York," all of 32 guns; the "Connecticut," the "Boston," the "General Green," of 36 guns; the "Siren" and "Argus," of 16 guns, and the "Enterprise," 14 guns. All ships "must claim your attention as well as your own," directed Secretary Stoddert.

The "Constellation" "cruised for about three months without finding any game," until she captured the "Insurgente," of 50 guns and 700 men of whom 350 were killed or wounded. The "Constellation" met a French, 74, later but the enemy being of superior force the "Constellation" "got out of reach." The next day the "United States" met the same French vessel and after an exchange of a few shots, Captain Barry also thought it advisable to withdraw, as his ship had become "dismasted" and had to go to Bermuda for repairs, while the "Constitution" was "much disabled in her mast and spars." Later Captain Nicholson captured the "Carteret," packet "and took her to St. Pierre" and again chased a French privateer into a harbor near that port.

The Story of Commodore John Barry

On February 30, 1799, the "United States," under Barry, gave chase to a French privateer. A well-aimed 24-pound shot was sufficient to "cut the career of the privateer short," for the ball went through her hull so that she quickly began to fill and settle. Captain Barry ordered the boats of his frigate to the rescue of the crew. Midshipman Stephen Decatur being in the first boat to reach the wreck and rescue the crew. "They were plaintively imploring for help," wrote an eye-witness, "with earnest gesticulations, not only from men but from God and although it is 'true they had abolished all religion they had not, it seemed, forgot the old way of invoking the protection of the Omnipotent.'"

The vessel was the "Amour de la Patrie," of 6 guns and 80 men. All her crew were saved. The "United States" also captured the "Tartufe," of 8 guns and 60 men. Desiring to relieve himself of his prisoners and hoping to make exchange of Americans imprisoned at Guadeloupe, Captain Barry sailed to Basse Terre flying a flag of truce, but was fired on by the French batteries. Hauling down the flag Barry returned the fire and battered the walls so effectively that the marks of the American shot were visible for many years. The "Merrimac," Captain Moses Brown, captured "Le Bonapart le Phenix," 14 guns, 128 men, and "La Magiciene," 14 guns, 63 men. The "Portsmouth" took "La Bonapart" (No. 2), "Le Bullante," "Le Tripon" and "Le Bon Peré," of 6 guns and 52 men. Seven other captures made by the squadron.

It is not within the scope of this narration to record the operations of the fleet or the exertions of the several commanders of the respective vessels composing it, but much that was creditable to our naval forces was done though little that could be called brilliant or conspicuous, beyond the capture of the "Insurgente" by Truxtun and the "Amour de la Patrie" and "Tartufe" by Barry. The main service of the fleet was in protecting our merchant vessels and convoying them to safe waters.

Commodore Barry was not in good health while on this expedition. This, the Secretary of the Navy, writing to him, 15th March, 1799, chose to "attribute to vexation for not being able to fall in with the French" than to the effects of the climate. He had the "most entire confidence" that when joined by the other vessels Barry would "afford the greatest possible protection to our commerce and punish the depredation on it."

Barry had been joined by the "Constitution," the "Washington" and the "Merrimac" and would later have under his command the "Portsmouth," the "Herald," the "Pickering," the "Diligence," the "Scammel" and the "Eagle." Secretary Stoddert notified him, and also that if his health obliged him to return, Captain Truxtun would take command of the fleet and of the operations.

On St. Patrick's Day, 1799, Captain Barry was at Prince Rupert's Island. The Hibernian Society of Philadelphia for the Relief of Emigrants from Ireland were, the same day, at dinner at Shane's Tavern and drank to the toast of

"COMMODORE BARRY AND THE NEW NAVY."

On April 8, 1799, Captain Barry was at Bridgetown, Barbadoes. For that port he had, as the youthful Captain of the schooner "Barbadoes," sailed from Philadelphia on October 2, 1766, almost a third of a century previous. What thoughts must have moved him we may conjecture at the change in his own circumstances and in that of the country of his adoption which had taken place. Then, at twenty-one, he was commander of his first vessel, a trading schooner of 60 tons. He had since made effective war upon the enemy of his native land and of his adopted country. He now entered Bridgetown the commander of a squadron of the chief armed vessels of his country. During the War for Independence he had acted in cooperation with French naval forces, now he was protecting the commerce of his country from the depredations of the French and inflicting punishment upon such as came in his path. He had made war on British naval vessels and taken captive many as well as those of England's merchant marine. Now he and his country were acting in accord with England in opposition to and in restraint of the French.

Friends had become enemies and enemies had become friendly, so much so that a Barbadoes paper, on his arrival there, could declare: "Whatever good fortune attends Commodore Barry will but increase the public esteem which he already possesses, as to see merit rewarded is the generous wish of every British bosom."

What a change!

This praise arose from the fact that Barry meeting the French privateer "Democrat" took from her the British Letter-of-Marque, "Cicero," which had been captured by the "Democrat." The darkness debarred Barry from capturing the "Democrat" also. The "Cicero" was of 450 tons and 50 men. Her Captain and three of the crew had been killed and thirty-six wounded. She had been in possession of the French for thirty-six hours when retaken by the "United States" with the prize crew of thirty taken prisoners. These he left at Guadeloupe in French possession. As there were no American prisoners there Barry thought it better to do so than to have them on the "United States" frigate "to eat more than they were worth."

On April 15, 1799, the Navy Department recalled the "United States," the "Constitution" and the "Washington," "with all possible expedition." The other vessels were left in command of Captain Truxtun. Barry, in the "United States," arrived at New Castle, Delaware, May 9, 1799, and within a month at the opera it was sung that "the gallant Barry" was "by all Columbia's sons adored." He was then in Philadelphia after leaving Lieutenant Charles Stewart in charge of the frigate. Barry was, on 13th May, directed to discharge the crew whose time expired that or next month, so as to give them "an opportunity of spending their money," that they might the sooner re-enlist for another year. Officers were directed "to open rendezvous for recruiting a crew." In the meantime Captain Truxtun had arrived at Norfolk and was received with "every mark of respect and attention." Captain James Barron was there also, but on June 2d Barry requested his return to Philadelphia as necessity obliged his presence, as the President had directed the Secretary of the Navy to send "us as soon as possible to protect our defenceless coast." Lieutenant Stewart, almost daily, sent reports of the overhauling work going on preparing the frigate for a voyage. The French privateers were active along the coast harassing the merchantmen, and so audacious as even to enter our harbors.

This made "the public mind very uneasy." So on June 29th the frigate sailed under orders to cruise along the coast to Charleston and after remaining there "long enough to let the citizens know" he was "in the vicinity"; he was to "proceed further south, indeed as far as the River St. Mary's," if he could return to Hampton Roads by the middle of July, where the "Constitution," Captain Talbot, would join the "United States," as it was intended to send both to the coasts of France and Spain. This did not come to be, however, as it was found necessary to have the vessels in the West Indies as soon as they could operate there.

Barry received "the President's command" that "taking the 'Constitution' with you, you proceed on a cruise to the Western Isles, to Madeira and Teneriffe and thence returning by Cayenne, Surinam and the Windward Islands, and reaching Guadeloupe about the middle of October where further orders would be handed" him. Then both frigates were to proceed to San Domingo and enter the port of Cape François, so they might be seen by General Touissant with whom and the people he was to "endeavor to cultivate a good understanding." After remaining two or three days there he was to return to New York, leaving Captain Talbot in the "Constitution" at San Domingo to take command of that station. Barry was given leave, however, if time did not permit his going to Madeira and Teneriffe as well as the Western Isles, he might proceed no further than the Western Isles.

"The protection of our commerce is the great object of the naval armament," said the Secretary, but on July 27th he notified Barry, "the projected enterprise to Europe must be given up," the frigate "United States" had to "remain on our coast for our protection at home." The "Constellation" was to be employed in the same way.

Barry was to "proceed from Hampton" southward as far as St. Mary's River and thence back along the coast and take the best chance of falling in with the enemy until about September 10th, when he was to return to New York if the frigate could pass the bar—if not then to proceed to Newport, to which latter he did, where he remained until sailing for France.

"On October 20, 1799, from Newport Harbor, R.I., Captain Barry notified the Hon. Jonathan Dayton, of New Jersey, that Owen Smith whom he had recommended as a midshipman for frigate 'United States' had, in many instances, 'behaved himself in a manner very unbecoming a gentleman, and as I conceive it my indispensable duty to prevent every person of bad conduct from getting a footing in the infant navy, I have, at his own request, discharged him. Your nephew, Mr. Williamson, has been too tenderly brought up to follow sea life; I think his father had better seek some other mode of life for him.'" (Crimmins' MS.)

The cruise ordered took six weeks, but no record of captures appears. The coast had been protected. That was the end to be obtained—not captures—as a formal declaration of war had not been made by either the United States or France. Though commonly called "the War with France" because of actual hostilities having taken place, officially, war did not exist between the two countries. It is not necessary for our purpose to detail the political course of the two nations with respect to the difficulties between them, but when negotiations had so far progressed that special Commissioners or Ministers were to proceed to France with a view of arranging a treaty, Captain Barry was, on October 16, 1799, notified that "the President has decided that the 'United States' shall carry our envoys to Europe and you will hold yourself in readiness to perform that service by the first of November at the farthest."

The envoys were Chief Justice O. Ellsworth, R.W. Davis, ex-Governor of North Carolina, and W.V. Murray, U.S. Minister at The Hague—"Envoys Extraordinary to the French Republic."

Captain Barry had orders to land them at any part of France they preferred and to touch at any ports they desired. Captain Barry was indeed on an old service. He had carried Colonel John Laurens and Lafayette to France to seek aid for America. Now he carried American envoys to demand justice for American commerce and the cessation of hostile measures against its freedom.

The mission President Adams declared was sent at one of the "most critical, important and interesting moments that ever occurred" in American history. Again was Barry given the old order so often given him during his Revolutionary career: "You will not capture anything on the voyage. This is a mortification to which it is necessary that you should submit. I hope to salute you an Admiral on your arrival at Philadelphia."

Captain Barry performed the duty assigned him and landed the envoys in France. After long negotiations a Treaty of Peace, Commerce and Navigation was agreed to September 30, 1800, with the First Consul Bonaparte. It was ratified by the U.S. Senate February 3, 1801, by the French July 31, 1801, and proclaimed December 31, 1801.

Washington died December 14, 1799. On the 20th Captain Barry received from the Navy Department a General Order of President Adams that all vessels should be "put in mourning one week by wearing their colors at half-mast high." The officers to "wear crape on the left arm below the elbow for six months."

During the year 1800 the "United States" frigate was not in active duty—the trouble with France having ceased, other occasions for her services did not arise. Lieutenant Mullowney was promoted to the command of the "Ganges" and thirty-five of the seamen of the "United States" transferred with him.

On July 16, 1800, Lieutenant Charles Stewart was given command of the "Experiment," Captain Barry expressing the hope that "he will be more active than he was," a hope which was justified in his subsequent career. At this time Barry's vessel was undergoing repairs. He wrote the Secretary, "she will not be out of the carpenter's hands until October." When she was ready for sea, Barry was directed "to proceed to St. Kitts and assume command of your squadron on the Guadeloupe station, taking under your convoy any merchant vessels ready to proceed for the Windward Islands; you have to protect our commerce to all the Islands and to guard our merchant vessels against all depredations from Porto Rico as well as from Guadeloupe and other dependencies of France." Later the Treaty of September 30, 1800, arrived, when Barry was directed to "treat the armed vessels of France, public and private, exactly as you find they treat our trading vessels."

Up to that time seventy-four French vessels had been taken and more than eighty had been retaken from the French. This was regarded as ample proof of the value of a Navy and made its advocates so jubilant that "What think ye of the Navy now?" was tauntingly asked of its former opponents.

So again Captain Barry's services as Head of the Navy were conspicuous and useful. But the Federalists, the party of Washington, of Adams and of Barry, were defeated by the election by the House of Representatives of Thomas Jefferson.

Reform and Retrenchment were the chief policies of his administration. With the measures against France, Jefferson's Republicans had had no sympathy. Their antipathy to Great Britain and their fury against Jay's Treaty were terrific. The new Congress of Jefferson ordered the cessation of work on the 74-gun ships, for which timber had already been collected. Only a quarter of a million of dollars was appropriated for naval expenditures. All but thirteen of the ships were sold. The new Navy established by the Act of 1794 was, within seven years, almost non-existent and would have been wholly so if the policy of the Jefferson Republicans had been fully carried out. Though that practically came to pass by the "laying up" of all vessels.

The Story of Commodore John Barry

Jefferson was inaugurated March 4, 1801. On the 23d of that month Captain Barry was notified to "call home all the ships in the West Indies. You are to make the best of your way to Philadelphia."

At the end of April the frigate "United States" was in the Delaware River and, on May 1st, the new Secretary of the Navy, General Dearborn, instructed Barry to bring the "United States" to Washington, "where it is intended she shall be laid up." There were now Navy yards at Portsmouth, N.H.; Charlestown, Philadelphia, Norfolk and Washington, in accordance with the advice Captain Barry had given in 1798 that such should be established and a Navy Department created.

Captain Barry sailed the frigate to Washington and on May 23d reported his arrival in the Potomac, "though his friends had declared that the President was not aware of the difficulties that would be met in getting the frigate there," as Mrs. Barry wrote the Captain the day he had arrived near Washington.

The first frigate of the New Navy was "laid up"—was at rest—had ceased operations, not because its usefulness was at an end and it might no more be serviceable, nor would there be occasion for her power as a protector of American commerce, but because the political policy of the Party in power did not sanction the possession of a Navy.

So having fulfilled its mission and its commander having obeyed instructions and brought the first born of the new Navy to the new Capital of the new nation he was, on June 6, 1801, notified:

"You have permission to retire to your place of residence and there remain until the government again requires your services."

The frigate "United States" served our country well in the War with France, in the War with Great Britain, 1812-15, and in subsequent duties, warlike and peaceful, until the War between the States, 1861-65, when while laid up "in ordinary" at the Norfolk Navy Yard she was, by the Confederates, sunk to obstruct the channel. After the war she was raised and in January, 1866, broken up, though Commodore Hitchcock endeavored to have her preserved, saying "if her value were only measured by dollars it may be unwise to attempt her preservation, but ideas and sentiments cannot be judged by such a standard. What is the use of being rich and great and powerful if we cannot afford to indulge becoming sentiments and cherish the memory of the bright deeds of our history." But she was broken up. All that remains as visible objects of her are two of her guns on the exhibition grounds of the Navy Yard at Portsmouth, Va.

The Navy was, on June 11, 1801, by President Jefferson, put on "a peace establishment." Of the Captains nine were retained, of Lieutenants thirty-six and of Midshipmen one hundred and fifty. Captain Barry was "one of those retained," he was notified. Half-pay was allowed from July 1, 1801.

Captain Barry's health was now failing. On returning to Philadelphia he was, in November, 1801, engaged in proving guns cast by Mr. Lane. The next year when directed to prove cannon at Colonel Hughes' works near Havre-de-Grace, Maryland, Barry's health did not permit him to go. On August 19, 1802, Barry, Dale and Bainbridge were appointed a Board to examine applicants for admission to the Navy—the Barbary Powers were again giving trouble to our merchant traders and imprisoning American seamen, and an idea that a more vigorous navy was needed and that paying tribute in money was degrading was gaining headway even among the Republicans. So that on December 22, 1802, the Secretary of the Navy notified Captain Barry, "We shall have occasion to keep a small force in the Mediterranean and we shall expect your services on that station." But the old Warrior-Sailor was nearing another Station. Ill health was enfeebling him, destroying his wonted activity. The flame of the fire of his ardor to serve his country was flickering so much as to remind him that death might be nearing.

So on February 27, 1803, he made his will. During the summer at his country residence at Strawberry Hill in the Northern Liberties he remain incapacitated for any further sea or other services useful to

The Story of Commodore John Barry

the country, or beneficial to mankind in general. He died September 13, 1803, and was buried from his City home on Chestnut Street below Tenth, south side, then No. 186. He was interred at St. Mary's graveyard the next morning, according to the custom of those days. St. Mary's was the church where Commodore Barry "was a constant attendant when in the City," as Bishop Kenrick wrote Colonel B.U. Campbell, of Ellicott Mills, January 15, 1844. [Balto. Archives, C.D. 14.] His estate amounted to $27,691. He is buried within a few feet of the entrance to the graveyard in the rear of the church. In the grave with him his two wives are interred—Mary died in 1771, Sarah in 1831.

Beside him northward lies his friend Captain John Rosseter, also of the County of Wexford, Ireland.

At the head of his grave to the northward is interred Captain Thomas FitzSimons, a signer of the Constitution of the United States, an officer in the Revolution, a merchant of Philadelphia and Representative in Congress.

Also at the head of Barry's grave, southward, lies the mortal remains of George Meade, a patriot of the Revolution and a merchant of Philadelphia.

This is the most Catholic Irish-American historical plot of ground in the United States.

Three of these patriots were born in Ireland—George Meade, born in Philadelphia of Irish parents.

Dr. Benjamin Rush, a signer of the Declaration of Independence, wrote the first draft of the epitaph for the tomb of Captain Barry. It read:

> Let the Patriot, the Soldier, and the Christian,
> Who visit these mansions of the dead,
> View this monument with respect.
> Beneath it are interred the Remains of
>
> ### John Barry
>
> He was born in the County of Wexford in Ireland,
> But America was the object of his patriotism,
> and the theatre of his usefulness.
>
> In the revolutionary War which established the
> independance of the United States, he
> bore an early and active part, as a Captain in this navy, and
> afterwards became its Commander in Chief.
> He fought often; and once bled in the cause of freedom.
> His habits of War, did not lessen his
> virtues as a Man, nor his piety as a Christian
> The numbers and objects of his Charities will be
> known, only at that time, when his dust
> shall be reanimated, and when he who sus in secret,
> Shall reward openly.
> In a full belief of the doctrines of the gospel,
> he peacefully resigned his Soul into the arms of his
> Redeemer.
> on the 13th of September 1803 in the 59th year of his age.
> His affectionate Widow hath caused this marble to be
> erected to perpetuate his name, after the hearts of
> his fellow Citizens have ceased to be
> the living Records
> of his public, and private Virtues.
>
> B. Rush

The Story of Commodore John Barry

Let the Patriot, the Soldier and the Christian
who visits these mansions of the dead
view this monument with respect

Beneath it are interred the remains of

JOHN BARRY

He was born in the County of Wexford in Ireland
but America was the object of his patriotism
and the theatre of his usefulness.

In the Revolutionary War which established the
Independence of the United States he
bore an early and an active part as a Captain in their
Navy and after became its Commander-in-Chief.

He fought often and once bled in the Cause of Freedom.

His habits of war did not lessen his
Virtues as a Man nor his piety as a Christian.

He was gentle, kind and just in private life,
was not less beloved by his family and friends than by
his Grateful Country.

The number and objects of his charities will be
known only at that time when his dust
shall be reanimated and when He who sees in secret
shall reward openly.

In the full belief in the doctrines of the Gospel
he peacefully resigned his soul into the arms of his
Redeemer

on the 13th of September, 1803, in the 59th year of his age.

His affectionate widow hath caused this marble to be

The Story of Commodore John Barry

ERECTED TO PERPETUATE HIS NAME AFTER THE HEARTS OF HIS
FELLOW-CITIZENS HAVE CEASED TO BE
THE LIVING RECORD OF HIS PUBLIC AND PRIVATE VIRTUES.

As cut on the tombstone after revision the epitaph was substantially the same. "Interred" was changed to "deposited"; "theatre" was stricken out and "aim" inserted and "honor" added after "usefulness"; "became" was changed to "was"; "Virtues as a Man" was made to read "the power of the virtues which adorn private life"; "charitable" was added after "just" and the sentence relating to the number and objects of his charities stricken out; "in the 59th year of his age" was omitted.

TOMB OF COMMODORE BARRY, ST. MARY'S GRAVEYARD,
PHILADELPHIA

In 1876, the original tomb having fallen into decay, a new tomb—the present one—was erected by contributions of the members of St. Mary's Church. The epitaph having become illegible the compiler of this record supplied a copy of the epitaph as it had been cut on the first stone. But Rev. Wm. F. Martin, the Pastor of the church, had the epitaph cut so as to read, and now may be seen, as follows:

The Story of Commodore John Barry

SACRED TO THE MEMORY OF COMMODORE JOHN BARRY, FATHER OF THE AMERICAN NAVY.

LET THE CHRISTIAN, PATRIOT AND SOLDIER WHO VISITS THESE MANSIONS OF THE DEAD VIEW THIS MONUMENT WITH RESPECT AND VENERATION.

BENEATH IT RESTS THE REMAINS OF JOHN BARRY, WHO WAS BORN IN THE COUNTY WEXFORD, IRELAND, IN THE YEAR 1745.

AMERICA WAS THE OBJECT OF HIS PATRIOTISM AND THE AIM OF HIS USEFULNESS AND AMBITION.

AT THE BEGINNING OF THE REVOLUTIONARY WAR HE HELD THE COMMISSION OF CAPTAIN IN THE THEN LIMITED NAVY OF THE COLONIES.

HIS ACHIEVEMENTS IN BATTLE AND HIS RENOWNED NAVAL TACTICS MERITED FOR HIM THE POSITION OF COMMODORE AND TO BE JUSTLY REGARDED AS THE FATHER OF THE AMERICAN NAVY.

HE FOUGHT OFTEN AND BLED IN THE CAUSE OF FREEDOM, BUT HIS DEEDS OF VALOR DID NOT DIMINISH IN HIM THE VIRTUES WHICH ADORN HIS PRIVATE LIFE.

HE WAS EMINENTLY GENTLE, KIND, JUST AND CHARITABLE AND NO LESS BELOVED BY HIS FAMILY AND FRIENDS THAN BY HIS GRATEFUL COUNTRY.

FIRM IN THE FAITH AND PRACTICES OF THE ROMAN CATHOLIC CHURCH, HE DEPARTED THIS LIFE ON THE 13TH DAY OF SEPTEMBER IN THE 59TH YEAR OF HIS AGE.

IN GRATEFUL REMEMBRANCE, A FEW OF HIS COUNTRYMEN, MEMBERS OF ST. MARY'S CHURCH AND OTHERS HAVE CONTRIBUTED TOWARDS THIS SECOND MONUMENT, ERECTED JULY 1ST, 1876.

REQUIESCAT IN PACE.

STATUE OF COMMODORE BARRY, FAIRMOUNT PARK, PHILADELPHIA

In the Centennial year, 1876, the Catholic Total Abstinence Union of America erected in Fairmount Park, Philadelphia, at the foot of George's Hill, a fountain costing $55,000. One of its five statues of heroic size is that of Commodore John Barry. The sides of the base contain inscriptions as follows:

The Story of Commodore John Barry

On the east:

> JOHN BARRY,
> FIRST COMMODORE
> OF THE
> UNITED STATES NAVY.
> BORN IN 1745
> IN WEXFORD COUNTY, IRELAND.
> DIED SEPTEMBER 13TH, 1803,
> AT PHILADELPHIA.

On the west:

> DURING THE REVOLUTIONARY WAR HE DISTINGUISHED HIMSELF GREATLY. HE FILLED THE VARIOUS COMMANDS ENTRUSTED TO HIM WITH SKILL AND GALLANTRY. WHEN UNABLE TO FIGHT ON THE OCEAN HE OBTAINED COMMAND OF A COMPANY OF VOLUNTEERS AND FOUGHT AGAINST THE ENEMY ON LAND.
>
> AMONG HIS EXPLOITS WAS THE CAPTURE, UPON MAY 29TH, 1781, OF TWO ENGLISH VESSELS, THE ATALANTA AND TREPASA, AFTER A HOTLY CONTESTED ACTION WITH HIS OWN SHIP, THE ALLIANCE.

On the north:

> IN JANUARY, 1776, HE COMMANDED THE BRIG LEXINGTON, THE FIRST REGULAR CRUISER THAT GOT TO SEA UNDER THE AUTHORITY OF THE CONTINENTAL CONGRESS AND THE VESSEL THAT FIRST CARRIED THE AMERICAN FLAG UPON THE OCEAN.

The Story of Commodore John Barry

On March 18, 1895, the Hibernian Society for the Relief of Emigrants from Ireland, now the Friendly Sons of St. Patrick, presented the City of Philadelphia a copy, by Colon Campbell Cooper, of Gilbert Stuart's portrait of Commodore Barry, to be placed in Independence Hall. Hon. Edwin Stuart, President of the Society and Mayor of the City and now [1908] Governor of Pennsylvania, presided and accepted the portrait on its presentation by General St. Clair Mulholland, who declared Commodore Barry to have been "one of the most illustrious of Ireland's sons, a brilliant child of the wind and waves, a heroic warrior of the sea who never knew defeat, the Father and Founder of the Navy of the United States. The Navy that from the beginning has been the admiration and model of all the nations of the earth."

On March 22, 1902, the torpedo boat destroyer the "Barry" was launched at the Neafie & Levy's shipyard. It was "christened" by Miss Elizabeth Adams Barnes, the great-great-grandniece of Commodore Barry and daughter of Captain John S. Barnes, U.S. Navy, retired, of New York City.

In July, 1902, Hon. M.E. Driscoll, of Syracuse, New York, proposed a Bill in the National House of Representatives appropriating fifty thousand dollars "to erect in Washington a monument inscribed

"JOHN BARRY
"THE FATHER OF THE AMERICAN NAVY."

At that and the next Sessions of Congress the Bill did not, in either Session, pass both Houses, but in the Session of 1906 it passed and was signed by President Roosevelt.

A site near the new Union Depot has been selected and, after the delay, usual in all governmental monumental projects, the monument will stand in a most conspicuous location in the Capital of the Nation.

STATUE OF COMMODORE BARRY, INDEPENDENCE SQUARE, PHILADELPHIA

On March 16, 1907, the Friendly Sons of St. Patrick of Philadelphia presented to the City of Philadelphia the bronze statue of Commodore Barry which now stands in Independence Square. It cost $10,500: was designed and executed by Samuel Murray, sculptor, of Philadelphia. General St. Clair Mulholland, on behalf of the Committee, presented the statue to the Friendly Sons of St.

Patrick. Rear Admiral Melville, U.S. Navy, retired, presented it to the City. It was accepted by Hon. John Weaver, Mayor of the City, who had signed the Bill passed by the City Council, permitting the erection of the statue in the Square.

CPSIA information can be obtained
at www.ICGtesting.com
Printed in the USA
LVHW031948270521
688710LV00005B/143